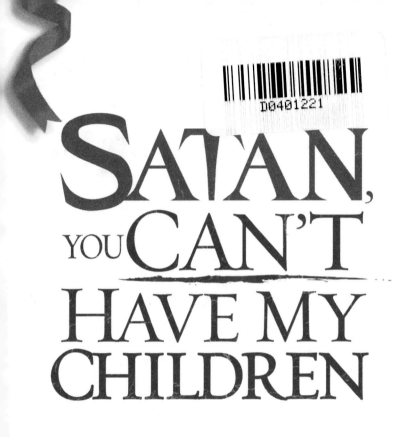

SATAN, YOU CAN'T HAVE MY CHILDREN

IRIS DELGADO

CHARISMA
HOUSE

Most CHARISMA HOUSE BOOK GROUP products are available at special quantity discounts for bulk purchase for sales promotions, premiums, fund-raising, and educational needs. For details, write Charisma House Book Group, 600 Rinehart Road, Lake Mary, Florida 32746, or telephone (407) 333-0600.

SATAN, YOU CAN'T HAVE MY CHILDREN by Iris Delgado
Published by Charisma House
Charisma Media/Charisma House Book Group
600 Rinehart Road
Lake Mary, Florida 32746
www.charismahouse.com

Cover design by Justin Evans
Design Director: Bill Johnson

Visit the author's website at www.crownedwithpurpose.com.

Library of Congress Cataloging-in-Publication Data:

Delgado, Iris.
  Satan, you can't have my children! / Iris Delgado.
      p. cm.
  Includes bibliographical references.
  ISBN 978-1-61638-369-5
 1. Child rearing--Religious aspects--Christianity. 2. Spiritual
warfare. I. Title.
  BV4529.D458 2011
  248.8'45--dc22

                                    2011005140

Portions of this book were previously published as *Satan,
You Can't Have My Children*, copyright © 1995, ISBN
978-0-9644097-0-5.

11 12 13 14 15—9 8 7 6 5 4 3 2 1
Printed in the United States of America

ACKNOWLEDGMENTS

I WISH TO FIRST thank my husband, John, who watched and supported me during the years I struggled to birth this book. I truly am married to a man of God.

I also want to acknowledge and express my gratefulness to my two daughters, Kristine and Kathy, who inspired me to trust God with all my heart during the difficult years in their lives. Thank you for bringing joy into my life and for your willingness to have confidence in my counsel.

A very special thank-you to all my friends who prayed and travailed for me and my family during the difficult times. There's no doubt in my mind that God is very attentive to our prayers, and in His timing, He answers.

And last, but most importantly, I want to thank the Holy Spirit for being my Friend and constant Helper all the time!

I COULDN'T HAVE DONE IT WITHOUT YOU!

CONTENTS

Foreword by Joni Lamb xi

Author's Comments xv

1   Spiritual Warfare to Save Our Children

God's arm is not too short 1

    Weapons for Spiritual Warfare Are Powerful 4

    Living in a Divided Home 8

    A Table Is Prepared Before Us 14

    Avoid Controlling Prayers 18

    Children Who Hit and Attack Their Parents 21

2   The Parental Influence

A father's influence can determine the life of his child 25

    Parents, Be Good Examples 26

    Mothers, Be Vigilant 31

3   Acknowledge That Your Child Is More Than a Body

Spiritually nurture the spirit of your child 37

    Nightmares and Bad Dreams 44

    Mental Disorders 45

    Establish and Develop a Solid Foundation for Your Child 47

4   Your Children's Inheritance

How to form your children's character 49

    Celebrate Your Son's Masculinity 51

    Empower Your Children 53

Paraphrased Scripture Prayers Taken From the
Women of Destiny Bible 61

Communicate Love and Commitment to Your Children 63

5   Preparation to Enter Into the Enemy's Camp

Build up your faith..65

Don't Stop Serving..67

Testimony of Answered Prayer...69

A Very Important Secret 70

Passing Judgment 72

Guilt and Condemnation..74

Only in God's Presence 75

Warning...77

In the Midst of the Storm...79

Training Mighty Little Warriors 82

Binding and Loosing…Learn to Use the Keys of the Kingdom......85

The Destructive Effects of Lust and Pornography 88

6   Praying for Your Children

Scripture support for prayers for spiritual growth.........................93

Knowledge of Jesus at an Early Age 94

Hatred of Sin 94

Protection From the Enemy 95

Respect for Authority..95

Healthy Relationships 95

A Responsible, Excellent Spirit...96

Submission to God 96

God's Choice for a Spouse...96

Sexual Purity..97

Hedge of Protection..98

Angelic Protection...98

Growth in Wisdom..99

Protection From Pestilence and Destruction 99

Protection From Weapons Formed Against Them 99

Wisdom and Understanding..................................... 100

Strong in Spirit 100

Keeping of God's Commandments 101

To Honor the Lord 101

True Worshipers 101

Knowledge From the Word..................................... 102

7   Bringing Down Strongholds

Defeating the works of the enemy 103

The Hidden Secrets... 104

Demonic Attacks.. 108

"I Can't Forgive Those Who Hurt Me"................. 110

Redeemed From the Curse 113

Scriptures Related to Deliverance 117

8   God's Promises for Parents

Scripture praying for children young and grown.........................121

Prayer of Faith... 131

My Identity and Position in Christ........................ 131

Prayer for Despondent and Rebellious Children............... 135

Appendix A: Declaration of Faith 137

Appendix B: Prayer to Receive Jesus Christ as

Lord and Savior..139

FOREWORD

As parents, we have all had this moment: Your precious little one whom you love so much now stands in defiance. And then you hear those pouty little lips rebelliously let loose that dreadful word: "NO!" And so the battle begins—not a battle of wills, but one of setting boundaries and defining character. It's a battle that will continue to adulthood.

It is no secret; being a parent is a tough job! How many times have I heard a parent say, "If I had it to do all over again, I would have done it better." Or, "If I knew then what I know now, I would have done things differently." But before you start beating yourself up, let me stop you. The fact of the matter is that none of us are perfect. You are going to make mistakes along the way, and you will probably, on more than one occasion, drop the ball. But it is not too late. You can be a godly role model in your children's lives, and you can pour into your children the Word of God and equip them to make right choices regardless of their age or your past mistakes.

Sadly, many parents today didn't have a godly role model when they were growing up, and they're struggling with issues that stemmed from their childhood. Maybe your childhood was one of abuse, or your home was dysfunctional. Now you're a parent, and you find yourself frustrated. Perhaps you're not sure what a godly role model even looks like, or you might be dealing with a difficult child and feel powerless. Maybe you don't want to make the same mistakes your parents made, but you find yourself repeating some of the same patterns.

The good news is you can become the parent that will help your children grow to be the godly men and women they are intended to be. It's never too late to influence your children to love the Lord with all their heart or to teach them how to live a life that is full, abundant, and pleasing to God.

We've all heard the adage that knowledge is power, and in parenting, it is key—but only when you understand that the battle of parenting is not so much a battle but rather spiritual warfare. Dr. Delgado's book is filled with information that will help you to be a strong spiritual role model and parent who knows how to fight for his or her children. What a great blessing to have a book that is filled with knowledge learned from real-life experiences. You don't have to spend years of learning through your mistakes. Take the principles from this book and apply them, and you will find amazing strength and power that will make a difference in your children's lives.

Today is a new day. The battle is yours to win. Pray the scriptures that are in this book. It's never too late to do the right thing for your children. They may be toddlers, teens, or even grown and out of the house, but regardless of their age, praying Scripture will be a powerful tool that can make a difference in their life.

I have known Iris Delgado for many years as she has loved and served her family unselfishly. This is a subject she is passionate about because she understands the importance of God and family. You will be encouraged, inspired, and motivated to not give up on your children. Parenting is one of the most difficult challenges in life. Use this book as a guide, and see what God will do when you stand your ground and say, "Satan, you can't have my children!"

—JONI LAMB
PRESIDENT, DAYSTAR TV
HOST, *JONI SHOW*

AUTHOR'S COMMENTS

THE SCRIPTURES, ADVICE, and experiences contained in this book have been of great value to me and to my children. My prayer is that you will benefit in the same way that my family has benefited and has been blessed through the daily application of these scriptures and fervent prayers. God is faithful, and He will hasten His Word to perform it!

Never give up in the face of adversity. It is in the midst of adversity that we grow stronger. "The word of God is living and active" (Heb. 4:12)! Praying scriptures are some of the most powerful prayers you will ever pray. When you pray scriptures, you remind God of the truth in His Holy Word and His promises to which He binds Himself and all of His power. Pray these scriptures for your children—young and grown. Stand firm on the Word of God and resist the enemy. *For greater is Christ in you than he that is in the world.* (See 1 John 4:4.)We have been guaranteed victory in the name of the Lord Jesus Christ.

You must cast the spirit of fear out of your heart, "for God has not given us a spirit of fear, but of power and of love and of a sound mind" (2 Tim. 1:7, NKJV). You must trust God and His Word. Fear is one of the weapons used by Satan to stop Christian parents from engaging in spiritual warfare for the well-being of their children. Fear can hinder your children from fulfilling the potential that God placed in their lives when they were born. But a sound mind created by the awesome power of God can overcome any fear that Satan attempts to impose upon you or your children.

If your children need to be restored and delivered from rebellion and disobedience, you must immediately search your heart and plan to engage in spiritual warfare for them.

Apply these scriptures together with your prayers. As you do, the Holy Spirit will continue to show you other scriptures. Keep on trusting God and praying scriptures. You will rise above your circumstances. You will experience peace in the midst of adversity. God is a not a God of confusion but a God of peace. It is up to the parents to create a peaceful home.

No matter what your children or loved ones do, you will rest assured that God's power is greater than the power of the enemy over them. If God is able to turn the heart of the king in His hand, He surely can turn the heart of your children toward Himself.

> We will reap a harvest if we do not give up.
> —GALATIANS 6:9

CHAPTER ONE

SPIRITUAL WARFARE TO SAVE OUR CHILDREN

GOD'S ARM IS NOT TOO SHORT

Thus says the Lord: Restrain your voice from weeping and your eyes from tears, for your work shall be rewarded, says the Lord; and [your children] shall return from the enemy's land. And there is hope for your future, says the Lord; your children shall come back to their own country.

—JEREMIAH 31:16–17, AMP

THIS BOOK WAS born out of the school of personal experience. I have learned that no matter how well you rear your children and teach them God's precepts and principles of godliness, they have to choose to have a personal relationship with the Lord and to serve God.

Many of you who are reading this book have uttered many tearful prayers for the salvation and wholeness of your children. Be

1

of good cheer! God hears every prayer, and He collects every one of your tears. You can be assured that every tear shed on behalf of a loved one and every tearful prayer uttered to God finds its way into the loving heart of Father God. He is still on the throne, and He answers prayers according to His timing, not our timing.

His arm is not too short. His ear is not too far. His power is not limited, and His grace and mercy never run out. You serve a great and mighty God who is able to reverse the circumstances, remove the hindrances, replace what the locusts have destroyed, put in a pure heart, and renew a right spirit. He is able to direct the heart of a person.

> The king's heart is in the hand of the Lord…He turns it whichever way He wills.
>
> —Proverbs 21:1, amp

Can you imagine that?

My prayer is that your attitude toward the problem in your home will change. Parents establish the attitude of the home, and they determine whether or not it is a home of peace or a home of chaos. A Christian home should not be one of constant chaos. A peaceful home is a huge blessing from God. I believe that if you exercise your faith, your frozen dreams and hopes will be restored. God is waiting for you to trust Him and to yield every aspect of your life to Him. Continue to read, understand, and practice using the powerful Word of God. As you start practicing, you will see many changes in your life and the lives of your children.

It is useless to observe or compare your family or your children with other families. Some families seem to have perfect marriages, perfect children, and perfect lives. However, very few people know what happens behind closed doors.

You may have questioned God: "I've done everything according to the Word of God. I've been a godly example. I've demonstrated love. Why is my child rebellious? Why is it taking so long for God to answer my prayers?" Or you may say, "God, I blew it as a godly example to my children—is it too late? Is there still hope?" Yes, there is still hope in the unconditional love and mercy of God. Targeted prayers and spiritual warfare will greatly help you in the battle. God promises to defeat our enemies if we obey and trust Him.

You may yourself be a victim of a dysfunctional home, and you have reared your children to the best of your abilities. Now you need help, for yourself and for them. You might have adopted or fostered children or have stepchildren from a second or third marriage, children with walls and defenses that you feel unable to deal with.

Take heart: unconditional love can overcome every obstacle that your children may erect. But it takes complete faith in the love and power of God, faith in the truth of the Word of God, and faith in the power of speaking and praying the Word of God over your loved ones. Only then will you start to see changes begin in their lives.

You may have young children who need nurturing and shaping as they grow up. They are still impressionable and teachable, and you can still influence their lives in a positive way. Whatever your reasons are for the need of divine intervention in the lives of your children, this book is for you. God's Word never returns empty; it will do what it says it will do—if we believe and doubt not.

> So is my word that goes out from my mouth: it will not return to me empty, but will accomplish what I desire and achieve the purpose for which I sent it.
> —ISAIAH 55:11

Don't be moved or affected by what you see and what you hear from your children. Continue planting these godly principles of parenting into the lives of your children. Exercise your faith. Keep stretching it a little bit more each day. God will use every situation in your child's life as a testimony for His honor and for His glory.

WEAPONS FOR SPIRITUAL WARFARE ARE POWERFUL

Faith is our powerful key for overcoming the powers of Satan. Demonic forces will try to convince you that what you see in the natural with your physical sight is the ultimate truth. This is totally incorrect.

In the spiritual realm, faith has the power to change those things that are seen in the natural to things that are congruent with the Word of God. "We live by faith, not by sight" (2 Cor. 5:7).

One reason is that genuine faith in the heart of a believer has the power to change outward circumstances to a desired outcome.

> For though we live in the world, we do not wage war
> as the world does. The weapons we fight with are not
> the weapons of the world. On the contrary, they have
> divine power to demolish strongholds.
>
> — 2 Corinthians 10:3–4

As Satan wages war against man, one of his tools is the creation of spiritual strongholds. These strongholds cannot be destroyed by the flesh or by the carnal nature of man. They have to be pulled down through fervent intercessory prayers, praying scriptures, and other methods of spiritual warfare.

Satanic forces are stalking every family living on this earth. The enemy is the devil, who "prowls around like a roaring lion looking for someone to devour" (1 Pet. 5:8). He is the thief who "comes only to steal and kill and destroy" our loved ones (John 10:10). However, he is a toothless and impotent enemy. He tries to rob Christians of their very substance. Christian parents need to remember that Satan was soundly defeated by the sacrifice of Jesus Christ upon the cross. If you can remember that Satan is powerless, you will be able to use your faith and spiritual weapons to overcome any satanic attack upon you and your family.

Many Christians who have inherited wondrous gifts from God often behave like little children who are unaware of their eternal legacy. They continue to live impoverished and defeated lives. Satan delights in deceiving many Christians by frightening them away from faith in the Son of God and from acceptance of the Word of God.

The Holy Spirit has been directed by God to anoint us to use His powerful weapons.

A Christian parent needs to remember that the battle must be waged against the devil and demonic forces, and not against the person who is behaving in an ungodly manner. It is the devil who is the spiritual enemy. Spiritual warfare should not be waged against a mate, a child, a loved one, or a boss. The loved one should be treated with unconditional love, while Satan is being engaged in spiritual warfare. As a parent, you must not be complacent. You must wrestle with and wage spiritual war against Satan on behalf of your family.

> For our struggle is not against flesh and blood, but against the rulers, against the authorities, against the powers of this dark world and against the spiritual forces of evil in the heavenly realms.
>
> —EPHESIANS 6:12

It would be unwise to engage in an actual war without armor or weapons. It is equally unwise to engage in spiritual warfare without using the armor of God and spiritual weapons. In order to wage spiritual warfare successfully, a parent must continually submit himself to God, and he must continually resist the devil.

The disciple James tells Christians how to deal with the devil:

> Submit yourselves, then, to God. Resist the devil, and he will flee from you.
>
> —JAMES 4:7

When a parent is truly submitted to God, and when he is resisting the devil, then the devil must flee! Yes, the devil has no choice but to flee from a Christian parent who is truly and totally submitted to Almighty God.

You resist the devil by using the proper weapons God has already provided for you. God has guaranteed the victory through the:

- *Name of Jesus.* God responds positively to the name of Jesus.

- *Blood of Jesus.* The blood saves the believer from sin and empowers the believer against the wiles of the devil and against demonic forces.

- *Power of the Holy Spirit.* This power anoints the believer to do great things in the name of Jesus Christ.

- *Keys of binding and loosing.* God gives the keys of binding and loosing so that things bound upon the earth will be bound in heaven, and things loosed upon the earth will be loosed in heaven.

- *Power of praise and worship.* Praise leads the believer into worship with God, and worship brings the believer into the very throne room of God.

- *Effective prayer.* The prayers of the righteous are heard by and responded to by God.

- *Power of agreement.* God promises that where two or more are gathered in His name, He will be there with them (Matt. 18:20).

- *The Word of God.* The Bible instructs the believer in all aspects of life.

In our book *Authority to Destroy the Works of the Enemy*, you will learn how to use these powerful weapons in your daily life and in every situation. God has already made available to you a treasure of divine power and the ability to make you "more than a conqueror" (Rom. 8:37).Many believers continue to live in defeat, worry, anxiety, depression, and unbelief. They lack knowledge of who they are in God and what position and *identity* they have in Christ.

Many people live in defeat because they don't know any better. Lack of faith and trust in God has them living in defeat. Ignorance in this area leads to failures.

LIVING IN A DIVIDED HOME

I was reared in a *divided* Christian home. My mother was a godly woman who manifested the fruit of the Spirit. She had a gentle, kind, and submissive character. The light of Jesus was evident in her life and actions. On the other hand, my father was double-minded in all of his ways and actions. One side of him reflected darkness—a life of unbelief, intimidation, control, and abuse. The other side reflected moments of kindness, gentleness, and self-control.

He was also a good provider for his family, and he was respected by almost all who knew him. My dad was a victim of the works of the enemy. He behaved irrationally because he was subjected to evil spirits.

Sadly, most abusers only abuse and mistreat their loved ones or those who are very close to them. The Bible says, "By their fruits you will know them" (Matt. 7:20, NKJV). It also says that a "double-minded man" is "unstable in all his ways" (James 1:8, NKJV).

During my research in spiritual warfare, I discovered that most characteristics, whether good or bad, are inherited, learned in the home, or passed down from one generation to another. The good news is that we can appropriate our freedom in Christ Jesus by the power of God's Word and the blood of Jesus Christ.

To *appropriate* means "to take possession of, secure, allocate, assign, appoint, and so forth." God wants us to take possession of all of the kingdom's rights and benefits that He has already deeded and guaranteed to us. We have been delegated power and authority over *all* the power of the enemy. I firmly believe that lack of knowledge will keep a Christian from enjoying the blessings and the peace of God.

Even though my mother was a devout Christian, she lacked knowledge in the area of spiritual warfare. Many Christians have been reared in a Christian home, and they have learned what the Word says about salvation, obedience, and holiness. But, unfortunately, I have discovered that many Christians are totally ignorant of who Satan is and what his devices, schemes, and strategies are against all believers in Christ.

My search for truth about this subject began when I heard testimonies of deliverance and of God's supernatural power to destroy strongholds in people who were bound and defeated by the enemy. It all started a few years ago when I visited my parents' home during Thanksgiving. I remember sitting down with my brother and talking with him about old times. This brother was addicted to drugs for many years.

Evident upon his young and handsome face were the effects of a hard and fruitless life. It saddened me to think how this very intelligent, young, and personable young man I was facing could allow himself to be driven by the miseries and slavery of drugs. He was driven by something stronger than he was.

The slavery of Satan can lead people to do things that stop them from leading healthy and normal lives. Living in a divided home set the pace and the example for my brother to choose wrong relationships and to turn to drugs as a form of escape from the deep pain within him. Peer pressures were too great for him to handle, because he did not have the backup or the affirmation of a father. This lack of direction from a father made it easier for him to choose a life of irresponsibility.

As we talked, the conversation took a turn toward his spiritual condition and his feelings and beliefs about God. Suddenly I noticed a twitching in his eyes and a change in his voice. I became apprehensive and fearful. As I looked at him closely, I realized that a demonic entity was manifesting itself. The look in his eyes was evil, and the smirk on his face was unnerving. The enemy did not want my brother to receive any counsel or encouragement from me. He wanted to keep my brother ignorant, bound, and defeated. I remember fumbling for an excuse to get up, and I quickly found myself standing in the kitchen trying to regain my composure.

Thinking about this experience on the plane as I headed back to Dallas, I remember thinking, "If the Bible says I have power and authority over all the power of the enemy, and I am more than a conqueror, why was I so scared and fearful over this incident?" Over the days and weeks that followed, I faced the truth: I was ignorant! I had no practice. All I had was a little head knowledge!

I had it! First Dad and his double-minded lifestyle, then Mom and her seeming helplessness, then my own suffering with the effects of child abuse and molestation, and now the thought of my brother—the fear of looking into his eyes at that evil thing glaring at me! I was just fed up. "God," I cried out. "Your Word says, 'I have given you authority to trample on snakes and scorpions and to *overcome all the power of the enemy*; nothing will harm you'" (Luke 10:19, emphasis added).

My quest took me to dozens of books, tapes, and seminars that were coupled with much prayer and seeking the face of God. I finally realized that the enemy had me deceived. I found new meaning in the words I had heard so many times: "Satan is defeated." "We are more than conquerors" (Rom. 8:37). "Resist the devil, and he will flee from you" (James 4:7). "The enemy is under your feet." "No weapon formed against you shall prosper" (Isa. 54:17, NKJV). "They overcame him [the devil] by the blood of the Lamb and by the word of their testimony" (Rev. 12:11).

Sound familiar?

The most powerful revelation to me was understanding my *identity in Christ*—I took it as a prescription from my Doctor Jesus. Three times a day I would confess who I am in Christ. Then I studied all about my spiritual weapons:

- ✦ The Word of God (in my heart and spoken)
- ✦ The power of the blood of Jesus
- ✦ The work of the Holy Spirit
- ✦ The keys of binding and loosing
- ✦ The power of praise and worship
- ✦ The power of prayers of agreement
- ✦ The power in the name of Jesus

I also studied at length the works of Satan and of all his workers of iniquity. I found out that he has long-term goals for all who claim Jesus as Lord.

My eyes were enlightened, and the blindfolds of deception and fear were removed from my eyes. The glory of God was revealed to my spiritual eyes, and I was able to understand my spiritual position of ruling and reigning here on this earth as a joint-heir with Christ Jesus. Once I knew in my mind, heart, and spirit what my identity, authority, weapons, position, and throne rights in Christ were, I took action. My life was revolutionized. I saw strongholds in my own life come tumbling down. I saw inherited traits broken.

Because of the abuse I experienced as a child and into my teen years, I had habits and thought patterns that were detrimental to me. They affected the way I acted, my decisions, my thoughts, and the lives of my loved ones. My parenting skills were in danger. Remember, a mother almost always sets the pace in her home.

What I thought was reality was indeed a distorted view of how I viewed life in general. I found out that many things in my mind needed to be cast off, revoked, and renounced. With the help of the Holy Spirit, I was empowered to bind and cast off all the thoughts, imaginations, habits, and things in my life that had been a hindrance to me and to others. These things were also hindering my spiritual growth and my freedom to live a victorious life.

As my mind was renewed by the Word of God, and as I confessed the truth, I began to unfold from a shy, timid, critical, fearful, and complaining person into a more sensitive, loving, kind, strong, and confident wife, mother, and person.

But I was not satisfied with the progress I had made. My goal was to see this work of deliverance and freedom working in the lives of my children, my husband, and my loved ones. God has been faithful to His Word. The compilation of the material in this book has been part of this growth. Everything you read here has been put to the test. The Holy Spirit has been my teacher and my guide.

My family has been the target of my spiritual aggression. This works, folks! God is ready to perform His Word when He finds one of His children who dares to believe that it works today!

Put it to the test yourself. Stand on God's Word. Confess and believe His promises. Don't dismay, and you shall enjoy the fruit thereof. Time after time I have seen God's Spirit through the power of His Word break through strongholds that looked impossible.

Satan is destroying families each day at an alarming rate. We must stand up and resist the enemy. Fight for your family! Stand in the gap. Your prayers are powerful. To resist is to take action; it is not being passive. It means you take a stand and don't budge, come wind or high water. You stand on God's promises while confessing His Word. When you do this, then God does the rest.

A TABLE IS PREPARED BEFORE US

God prepares a table before us in the presence of our enemies. Do you know why a table, and what is on that table? Do you know why it's set in the presence of our enemies? I believe that God provides everything that is necessary for our time of need!

All of the weapons and tools that you need for spiritual warfare can be found upon His table placed in the presence of our enemies. The Word of God that is alive and active is on that table! The table is not placed and set in your private bedroom—**NO!** It is placed and set in front of your enemies because that is when you need assistance and powerful weapons. It is also a table full of fatness and provision.

> You prepare a table before me in the presence of my
> enemies.
>
> —Psalm 23:5

The Holy Spirit brings to your remembrance the Word of God that is stored up in the tablet of your heart, the Word that you have studied, applied, tested, proven, believed, and confessed. *You are dynamite. You are a threat to Satan.* A believer who is equipped and who is no longer ignorant about spiritual warfare is a person who is armed, powerful, and fearless. Satan should not be a threat to you.

Folks, it is time to wake up, to take control, and to act. Learn from the Holy Spirit, confess the Word, and do not fear negative words. It is time to dress for action against the enemy. We should be defeating the enemy, not the enemy defeating us. Too many born-again believers sit defeated and emaciated in front of a treasure chest full of God's blessings, authority, weapons, anointing, and His transforming Word.

Sadly, too many children are imitating and receiving training from parents who are weak, stressed, depressed, and fearful. It is time to break loose from negative molds and traditions and from what is conceived to be reality but is really the lie of the enemy.

Reality is what we learn as truth. But that is not all truth. Much of it is distorted, depending upon what our parents learned and taught us, our values, boundaries, beliefs, and so forth. Reality is what we learn to be truth. But what we think is reality is not always the truth. Reality is found in the Word of God or the truth of God; it is the Bible that reveals what is real. It should be our guide, our manual, our example.

Much of what people believe is truth might be distorted. Distortion of truth is a legacy we receive from our parents or caregivers. Things taught by parents often become the attitudes, beliefs, and values of the children. As believers, we have the privilege of hearing and learning God's truth. As we apply God's Word, change begins to take place in our lives and in the lives of our family. The lives of our loved ones begin to reflect the truth of God.

Coming back to Mom, one day I said to her, "Mom, you need to add some very important things to your praying and spiritual warfare. I have learned that there are several kinds of prayers we can pray, but when I learned about warfare praying, I found that it dramatically changed and revolutionized my personal life and the lives of many others."

We have been given all power and all authority over all of the works of the enemy. We must direct that power and authority directly against any enemies who come against us. If Jesus wanted to do all of our spiritual warfare, He wouldn't have challenged us to wear the full armor as described in Ephesians 6 or delegated to us the authority to tread upon all of the power of the enemy.

The phrase *tread upon* means "to stomp, kick, pounce, and to beat." It doesn't mean to walk gingerly or to ignore totally. We must become aggressive in our warfare, especially when our loved ones are being negatively affected by the works of the enemy and the powers of darkness.

We tread upon demonic forces by using the Word of God, which is alive and active. We also use our keys of binding and loosing when we pray with authority and when we command the evil spirits to loosen their control of an adverse situation.

For example, one powerful spiritual command that you can say with authority is:

> *Spirit of fear and confusion, I command you out of my life* (or out of the life of your child or loved one). *In the name of Jesus, I bind your works and your strategies from hindering me with fear. I plead the blood of Jesus, and I declare that greater is Christ in me than all of the power of the enemy. Because I am a child of God, the evil one cannot touch me.* (It could be a spirit of infirmity, rebellion, lust, insatiable desires, fear, panic, or other spirit.)

Finally, my mother was able to pray with boldness and authority. She was able to see dramatic changes take place in the life of my father and in the lives of her loved ones.

At one point in my father's life, he suffered a car accident that left him a quadriplegic for fourteen years. During that time Mother suffered many sleepless nights and much torment. The

SATAN, YOU CAN'T HAVE MY CHILDREN

evil spirits tormented my father, especially during the night hours, and my mother was unable to sleep soundly.

I remember when she called me and said, "Dear Iris, you'll never know what the knowledge of my position in Christ is doing in this situation with your father. I am using my authority in the name of Jesus in order to bind these tormenting spirits that attack your father, and they are obeying my commands! I am sleeping better, and he is getting more rest."

I am only giving you a little sample of the wonderful victories Mom was able to experience as she became fearless and exercised her authority in the name of Jesus.

AVOID CONTROLLING PRAYERS

It is extremely important that we always begin praying with thanksgiving to God and for people who need our prayers. The apostle Paul, in almost all of his prayers for his fellow Christians, began with a positive prayer of thanksgiving for them. He knew that God was a God of love who loves unconditionally. It didn't matter how rebellious or sinful they were.

You can see the example of faith in God's power in 1 Corinthians 1:4–8. A positive attitude of faith is created as you start thanking God for "those things which do not exist as though they did" (Rom. 4:17, NKJV) in the person's life, even though you acknowledge their faults and problems. It is important to thank God for beginning to change things that are not into what they can be in Christ as we stand in agreement with God's Word.

Controlling prayers start by focusing on the negative and by asking God to change, sever, transform, stop, bind, and remove. They tend to bring upon the person a burden of guilt and condemnation. These are prayers that attempt to control and condemn. Many people are unable *to rise above* these prayers.

All prayers have an effect, just as our words have an effect. Whether in a positive or in a negative way, they will affect the person's attitude and the circumstances involved in the lives of those for whom we are praying.

In my own life I have learned to thank God for my children and for God's awesome plan for their lives. When I see a relationship develop that I feel in my spirit is not in God's will for them, I immediately enter into God's presence, and I thank Him for His perfect plan for them.

I pray in faith, trusting God to intervene in their lives. I refuse to be moved by what I see, hear, or feel. I confess and declare all of those good things that I expect to see manifested in their lives. Then I enter into spiritual warfare and praying scriptures.

I bind all rebellion and the strategies of the enemy from becoming effective in their lives. God will do the rest in His infinite mercy, time, and compassion for us.

We must take care not to become bitter and judgmental, even in our prayers. Sometimes we pray for God to sever a relationship, and God does so. Many times we see our loved one get involved in a worse situation. Learn to trust God with your children. Pray in a positive way with thanksgiving. Pray scriptures, not your own words. Allow God to be God.

When you allow the love of God to be manifested through you

to your children, it will be the greatest deterrent against sin and rebellion in your child. This deep love from you will be better than anything that your child can see or have. The greatest deterrent against sin and rebellion in your child is the love of God manifested in your love for your child.

When you feel like screaming, yelling, preaching, or scolding—**STOP!** Take a deep breath. This is the time for you to take control of your emotions, mind, and body by refusing to allow your feelings to rule your actions and your words. Reach out with God's love and kindness toward your loved ones. Be an example. Don't compromise your values or bend your rules, but act in love. Your child may become angry with you, but deep down in his heart he will begin to think that maybe you're right and maybe he is wrong. In God's timing, God's love in you will win out. Examine yourself to see if your prayers are meant to manipulate or to control. If they are, ask God to forgive you. Ask the Holy Spirit to teach you how to pray for your loved ones. It will dramatically change your life and the lives of others.

> Do not be anxious about anything, but in everything [every situation], by prayer and petition, with thanksgiving, present your requests to God. And the peace of God, which transcends all understanding, will guard your hearts and your minds in Christ Jesus.
>
> —PHILIPPIANS 4:6–7

CHILDREN WHO HIT AND ATTACK THEIR PARENTS

If your children are hitting or attacking you and their brothers or sisters, I have one direct and urgent word for you: **GET HELP!** Don't wait until it is too late and they take control of the family. A child should not rule or reign in the home. Authority to destroy the works of the enemy is given to Christian parents by God. Begin immediately applying the principles found in this book. These principles work and will bring about dramatic changes if you believe that God can do it through your obedience and prayers.

If your children are grown, and they still live at home without obeying rules, begin engaging in spiritual warfare. The power of God working in you is greater than the power of the enemy. Submit to God, resist the devil, and Satan will flee from you. This is a fact—a truth. Submission to God means total surrender to His ways and to His will. It is a total trust that He is capable and able to take care of that which concerns you.

When you practice trusting and believing the work of the Holy Spirit in you and in your family, you will begin to see changes and transformation. You will see and enjoy these positive changes in your children and in your family life sooner than you thought possible.

Most of the time the change has to begin in us. If we yell, they will yell. If we curse, they will curse. If we talk negatively, they will talk negatively.

When we change, they also will change. If this is not the case for you, then stand and resist. Your effective, fervent prayers will avail much. If you do find yourself in this situation, then determine to make changes.

Begin with your words, prayers, and thoughts. The Holy Spirit will be your helper and guide. Forget about the way you have done things in the past. Forget about your feelings, and walk by faith. Embark on a journey to wholeness that will restore your life and the lives of your family members. Satan does not have to take your children or your mind. God has enabled us to triumph and to overcome evil with good.

I close this chapter by encouraging you to seek God's Word about these principles and to consider applying them to your everyday life through prayer. I have been able, each and every day, to apply these principles in my life, my husband's life, my daughters' lives, and in the lives of countless others. I have seen miracles of deliverance from manic depression, sickness, disease, fear and torment, destructive thought patterns, rejection, unbelief, and wrong relationships.

Prepare your heart. If you submit to God with all of your heart, put on your spiritual armor (which is God's Word in your heart and in your mouth), and aggressively resist the devil, the devil will have to flee from you, your household, and from those for whom you pray. The key is to yield your life to God completely and to be obedient to His Word. Once you experience the love and the power of God in your life, you won't desire anything else. You will notice that I repeat the importance of obedience and trust throughout the chapters in this book. I don't want you to forget it, because without obedience and trust your efforts will be in vain.

Children have a sharp sense of what is right and wrong. They are also avid imitators of their parents. As parents change, they also change. There is no case too big or too impossible for God to change and transform. God's love in action through you can tear down the greatest strongholds and barriers in your family.

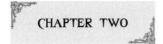
THE PARENTAL INFLUENCE

A FATHER'S INFLUENCE CAN DETERMINE THE LIFE OF HIS CHILD

*In a similar way, urge the younger men to be self-restrained
and to behave prudently [taking life seriously]. And show your
own self in all respects to be a pattern and a model of good
deeds and works, teaching what is unadulterated, showing
gravity [having the strictest regard for truth and purity of
motive], with dignity and seriousness. And let your instruction be sound and fit and wise and wholesome, vigorous and irre-
futable and above censure, so that the opponent may be put to
shame, finding nothing discrediting or evil to say about us.*

—TITUS 2:6–8, AMP

OUR CHILDREN CANNOT learn true love if what they see
and hear are anger and disagreement. Many parents
come from homes heartbroken because of sin and their
parents' and ancestors' iniquity. Some were abandoned and have

experienced pain and deep wounds. Others were attacked and are victims of sexual or mental abuse.

For God nothing is impossible. We are not victims! It's time to strip the old man and to tell Satan, "No more crumbs; Jesus Christ paid the price, and I'm free of the past! This curse will not continue to work in my family." It's time that parents reading these words become true men and women who believe in God. Stop the curse in your home! Your children do not have to follow in the footsteps of their ancestors or the sins of their parents. Stop the roots of irresponsibility. Leave a blessed legacy for your children and your grandchildren. Break the power of bondage and the generational curses. Become the whole, new creation Christ Jesus paid the price for us to enjoy to the fullest!

PARENTS, BE GOOD EXAMPLES

Father, teach your son how to be a whole man. Teach him to be a man, not a mama's boy. It all begins at home. Begin by asking forgiveness for the actions that have caused wounds and dysfunctional patterns in your children. A son needs affirmation, hugs, kisses, and his father's positive words. The son who doesn't receive his father's affirmation tends to be rebellious and disobedient and, in many cases, will never learn to love properly.

Teach your son how to treat his mother, sisters, and bride-to-be. The son must learn from his father that the mother is to be respected, honored, and treated delicately. The son needs to learn from his father how to treat his sisters. Many heartbroken young women have told me how they have been abused or manhandled by their fathers or brothers. It's time that fathers become true men of God and teach their children how to become men who respect women. The son will do with his wife what he has seen his father do with his mother.

What a big responsibility the father has!

Unfortunately, our world is full of men and women who are wounded, attacked, tormented, without values or limits, and looking for help from others who also need help and orientation. Cowardly men abandon their homes because of things that they themselves have permitted.

It's never too late to start over again. If God is willing to rescue us and make us a new creation, how much more should a father or a mother be willing to forgive and change? They too can start over again. It's time to declare, "Satan, you can't have my family!"

Let's look at some keys to healthy, effective fatherhood

Obviously, I am not a father. But I have observed many fathers, especially my husband. This section comes from careful observation in my forty years of marriage, parenting, and counseling.

A good father spends time with his children. In the same way that we work, make appointments, go to meetings, are members of different clubs, dine with our friends, and do many other things, we must take time to share and have fun with our children. Fathers, your son needs to spend time with you alone, either to play sports, go fishing, or to eat ice cream together.

Everything you would have wished that your father had done with you when you were a child, do together with your children. You will leave them with a treasure of memories. The time that you spend with them will be better than a monetary inheritance.

A good father loves, affirms, and cares for his wife and his children. Many women change drastically during their marriage. As a newlywed, the wife smiles, is warmhearted and kind, takes care of herself, and is probably fit. What happens with time?

Negligence brings drastic changes to the family. Both parents have a God-given responsibility to influence and be at the helm of their home. Each has a role to perform. When one neglects his or her duty, the couple begins to experience negative changes, and the children begin to suffer as they learn to absorb and imitate what they see. The solid foundation begins to crack, and the entire family suffers.

The husband and father who loves and cares for his wife and children will be the king of his home. Some women, no matter how well they are treated by their husbands, rebel and are dissatisfied with everything. Often I see that the wife or husband does not want to let go of the parents. In other cases of family discords, the root of the problem is a manipulating and controlling mother-in-law. The Bible says that manipulation is equal to sorcery. There should be a healthy separation between the parents and the couple and a complete union between the couple. If you do not have this healthy separation, you need help. God created the wife to respect and help meet the needs of her husband, and the husband to protect, respect, and love his wife. We are men and women capable of loving with all our hearts, but we must choose to do so.

The father who treats his daughters with respect and tact will have virtuous daughters who will become passionate and good-hearted wives. The father who does not respect his daughter will have a rebellious daughter with a wounded self-esteem. There are millions of them looking for acceptance.

The rejection and carelessness of a father toward his daughter create unstable behavioral patterns for life. When a daughter does not find love in her home, she will look elsewhere and will usually end up in the hands of someone with the same traits as her father and who will make her very unhappy.

The father who abuses his daughter is worse than a criminal. Surveys prove that men who abuse their daughters or sons come from different and diverse backgrounds. The more strict, harsh, and legalistic the man has been in his own home and church life, the more likely he will be an abuser. God heals and will have mercy on any man or woman who has problems with abuse and asks for forgiveness and help. We have this problem not only in the secular world but also in our Christian churches. I've counseled with many victims, daughters of ministers of progressive and admirable churches and ministries. Many men need help—men who abuse their children and their wives. And now, many women need help—women who abuse their children and themselves.

Incest and molestation is very common in many Christian homes today. It's surprising and troubling to hear of the great number of prostitutes and homosexuals who admit that they left their homes at a young age because of incest and repeated sexual abuse.

Abuse is now rampant. It used to be men who were known as

the abusers, but in today's society we are also hearing many news stories of women sexually or mentally abusing their own children. I personally have encountered this situation during counseling. I recently read in a magazine that a growing number of controlling and manipulative women mentally abuse their husbands. In reality, we need change and more information and training on this subject.

Fathers, please pay attention to the emotions and the thoughts of your children. Do not put all of your attention on how they look, dress, or how they dye their hair, paint on tattoos, and use makeup. What's in their hearts is what matters and what is important. Always guide your children toward God. Be a dynamic example, curious, good-humored, and always available for what they need, especially their emotional issues. You will be the person they are going to imitate. Teach them to confide in you, to be accountable, to make investments, to be good workers, to save money, how to put God above everything else, and to think big and positively.

What steps must be taken to improve family relationships?

1. The act of repentance before God and each other is the first step toward healing and change.

2. The second step is to join a group of believers who can bring guidance and accountability and promote discipline.

3. Making a commitment with your spouse and implementing a plan to change and walk in God's

love will be the third step toward the stability and
happiness of your family.

Satan has big expectations and plans for your family, but you
can change his plans and put into action all of God's promises for
your family. We all have to make choices. Some of them will be
difficult choices. *The more sacrificial a choice, the more value it has
and the more satisfaction it will produce to many generations.* Wow!
That's something to meditate on.

MOTHERS, BE VIGILANT

Do not allow your daughters to run around the house half naked.
Satan walks around like a roaring lion looking for someone to
devour and tempt. Do not enable your husband to be tempted by
your negligence at home, especially if weeks and months go by and
there's no sex life between you. Our young daughters need to be
taught early how to comport themselves at all times, never to sit
right in the middle of Daddy's lap, especially as they become toddlers and adolescents.

I was going to stop right here and continue with another topic,
but let me say a few more important things.

God created woman as a delicate vase and wants her to be han-
dled as such. I realize that many of you are being oppressed and
mistreated. Personally, I watched for many years as my father victimized my mom. But I also watched as I saw my mother refuse to
succumb to the attacks of the enemy through my father. She was
never a victim. She was a victor. How did she do it? She stayed

connected to her source: Jesus Christ. Her mind was always in prayer, even while she worked, cooked, and attended her family. She was thankful and kept a smile on her face. Was it difficult? Yes. I believe she maintained a 90 percent mental attitude and 10 percent physical.

Mom knew her position in Christ. She was unbeatable, because God sustained her. Today she is eighty-three years old, smiling, thankful, and prayerful.

What big picture do I see today among our young couples? I see a complete disarray instead of what a Christian home should be. *Confusion and disorder reign in too many Christian homes.* I'm thinking of five young couples right now. A young wife is unhappy because her husband has to work overtime almost every day, and her food gets cold and dry before he comes home. Give me a break! Millions of men would love to have his job right now. Another wife feels insecure because she is gaining too much weight and her husband is starting to make wisecracks. I will put this situation under the title of *disorder.* We can do something about this. We are temples of the Holy Spirit, and we must rule over our bodies. Not only do we get out of control in our weight, but so do our children. Ah, this book is about "Satan, you can't have my children"…not about food and marriage.

Confusion and disorder in our homes are the main reason why we have so many out-of-control children and young adults. They enter their marriages without the necessary survival tools and godly examples for a successful and healthy marriage. Perhaps my next book will be on marriage, and I will be able to expound and give some great counsel that I received from Mom and my wonderful grandmother. And now I have my own wisdom developed through forty years of a great marriage and the knocks and triumphs of life.

Moms, at home we should be *gentle as a lamb*, manifesting the fruit of the Spirit tenderly, with love and positive words. Do not be negative. Do not shout or scream. Do not gossip or speak ill of others. Speak life and not death. Speak blessings. Speak your blessings out loud. Our children are watching and hearing. Never criticize, especially the church leaders. Our children will think they are all hypocrites, and as they grow older, they will want nothing to do with church.

Maintain the spiritual temperature at home at a pleasant level. Women set the pace at home. We are like thermostats. If it's too hot or too cold, it will be uncomfortable. If we talk too much or nag and complain all the time, the temperature will be uncomfortable. Bless with words of encouragement. Pray in the Spirit. Think before speaking.

In the spirit, be "bold as a lion" (Prov. 28:1). Learn to pray, intercede, and wage war. Remain connected to the Holy Spirit.

Learn to recognize the danger signals: a bad-tempered, quiet, or serious spouse; a lazy, distracted, irate, unhappy, fearful, or rebellious child.

Learn to discern Satan's tricks: bad decisions, bad investments, money wasted, and disputes.

Pray for discernment. Pray with power. Pray fervently. Pray without losing heart. Pray all the time. Tie your heart, mind, and emotions to God's heart. Loose Satan's power and influence in your life. Loose all curses and Satan's plans for your family. Use your keys of binding and loosing.

Keep yourself constant, not cold or lukewarm. Be consistent and balanced. Activate your faith, creative talents, and gifts. Don't try to get out of the fire, but learn to pass through the fire.

God promises to be with you in all situations and at all times. Cultivate good-hearted friends who do not gossip or speak ill of others.

Keep the flames of love and sex burning. Do not neglect your conjugal intimacy. Keep your bedroom clean, inviting, and sweet smelling. Plan your intimacy ahead of time; change rituals with special details. Study the Song of Solomon. Be innovative and creative. Learn to be an admirer. It may be a little hard at the beginning, but it will reap great benefits in your husband's life and character as well as in your children's. Look for something to admire and compliment in your husband:

"You are God's gift to me and our children."

"You have a great body."

"You smell wonderful."

"You make me feel special."

And when he comes home smelling like an old dog and sweaty from work, tell him, "Honey, you smell good…you smell like money!" My husband really loved this one.

Although you don't like doing it because you are not used to saying or giving compliments, the more you practice, the more you will reap the benefits and feel the emotions of an intimate relationship.

Do not say, "You should admire and compliment me." One of us has to begin to change. You should start! The one that sows, reaps!

Take care of your body, health, and children. Learn to maintain a balanced diet. If you or your spouse needs to lose weight, I advise you to begin right away by not eating too much white bread, white rice, potatoes, or anything that contains white flour and sugar. Prepare a weekly menu of everything that you are planning on eating every day. Involve your family in the selection of dishes that they like. Balance your meals. Try to cook your food with vegetable or olive oil. Share your meal in a restaurant. Every three months, try doing a twenty-one-day Daniel fast. It's really awesome.

If your husband demands biscuits and gravy to eat every day, continue preparing them for him, but make the changes for you and your children. Once you get fit, you will not need as many of the things that you stopped eating. You will have more energy and strength.

This advice is given from my personal experience. After a long illness, incurable by a doctor's diagnosis, the only thing that helped me recover my strength was my confidence in the Word of God and a diet of the natural foods that God created for our health and sustenance. I stopped eating pork and fried foods and only ate cage-free chicken and wild fish three times a week. The restoration has been fabulous. A balanced diet and a life consecrated to God is the recipe for a healthy, peaceful, and harmonious life. God has created everything we need to be content and healthy.

Your children will grow strong and will imitate you for the rest of their lives!

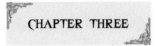

CHAPTER THREE

ACKNOWLEDGE THAT YOUR CHILD IS MORE THAN A BODY

SPIRITUALLY NURTURE THE SPIRIT OF YOUR CHILD

It is the Spirit Who gives life [He is the Life-giver]; the flesh conveys no benefit whatever [there is no profit in it]. The words (truths) that I have been speaking to you are spirit and life.

—JOHN 6:63, AMP

A CHILD IS NOT only a physical body but also a spirit being. Each one of us is a spirit. God is a Spirit. Jesus is a Spirit. The Holy Spirit is a Spirit. Satan is a spirit. Our spirit lives in a physical body.

Many Christians are not consciously aware that they are a spirit covered by a physical body. We feed our children, bathe them, dress them up, send them to school, and provide piano lessons, ballet classes, karate, and other sports. We take them to the dentist's and doctor's offices and so many other things that take care and nourish their bodies and intellect.

But what about their spiritual nourishment? Are we feeding their spirit being? It is our spirit being that needs knowledge, understanding, and guidance.

> But you are not living the life of the flesh, you are living the life of the Spirit, if the [Holy] Spirit of God [really] dwells within you [directs and controls you]. But if anyone does not possess the [Holy] Spirit of Christ, he is none of His [he does not belong to Christ, is not truly a child of God].
>
> —ROMANS 8:9, AMP

We all have a particular personality molded by our caregivers and life experiences.

It is of utmost importance that a parent pays attention to and is aware of the spiritual needs of the child. We accomplish this by creating and planning activities and narrating Bible stories that will develop a desire for spiritual things.

Here are some suggestions and examples that I practice with my grandchildren, which are producing good results.

Narrating Bible stories in a fun and creative way, such as the Bible story of David and Goliath. Have your child act out as David, swinging a slingshot (a sock with something soft in it) and aiming it at Goliath. You or a sibling can act out as Goliath who falls down when he gets hit by David. Explain how David's dependence on God, and his obedience to his parents, enabled him to be used by God and save his family and a whole nation.

Have your child memorize scriptures such as Psalm 23, the Lord's Prayer, the Ten Commandments, the Beatitudes, and other important portions of Scripture. I suggest using the reward method. Whether it's money, a toy, or throwing a party, we must be creative. A parent, grandparent, caretaker, or another sibling can make some quality time for your child and practice repeating over and over until your child has memorized the scripture(s). This endeavor is so important that it will have an everlasting spiritual effect on your child.

When my grandson was age nine, I helped him memorize Psalm 23 by rewarding him with twenty dollars toward a pair of tennis shoes he wanted. We practiced repeatedly until he got it. Now, four years later, I ask him to recite Psalm 23, and he still knows it by heart. I also explained to him the importance of reciting this psalm if he ever felt afraid or discouraged, or as a prayer before going to bed.

Every little bit of spiritual guidance you give your children will be as nuggets of gold in the spiritual banks of their hearts. I still remember the songs, psalms, proverbs, poems, stories, and Scripture verses my mom *made* me memorize as a child. What a treasure!

Teach your children how to make faith declarations, such as:

+ I am a child of God.

+ I can do difficult things with God's help.

- I will not fear because God is with me all the time.

- I am intelligent, and I will do well in school.

- Nothing is impossible with God on my side.

- The Holy Spirit is my Friend and my Helper—I can do this!

- I have the mind of Christ to make wise decisions.

- Christ Jesus lives in my heart.

Remember what I said in the beginning: Your child is not only a body. He is a spirit living in a physical body. We must nourish and feed the spirit just as we feed the physical body.

I once heard a story about two big and fierce-looking dogs. The owner would feed one dog a ration of dried dog food every day. The other dog got fed steak and a big bone. A thief came to burglarize the house, and the dog that was fed dried dog food cowered and whimpered in a corner. But the dog that was fed steak and bones pounced on the burglar, pinning him down until the owner came home. The moral of this story is that if you do not feed your child's spirit the triumphant Word of God and how to declare God's Word, he will not know how to act in the spirit realm when the enemy comes to attack. Instead of being fearless, he will be fearful.

> Submit yourselves, then, to God. Resist the devil, and
> he will flee from you.
>
> —JAMES 4:7

Teach your child how to pray *fervent prayers*, not just little bed-time and mealtime prayers. Here is an example of a fervent prayer your child can learn to say when he is ill:

> *Dear Abba Father, this is Gabe* [your child's name].
> *I know You hear my prayer. I believe that Jesus is my*
> *healer. I thank You for healing me and taking this fever*
> *away in the name of Jesus. Amen!*

Abba is *Daddy*. Teach your child to relate to Father God as his Daddy in heaven. It makes prayer an intimate relationship, one that he can practice in his prayer time.

Teach your child big and full-of-meaning words from the Bible. Not too long ago I was watching one of the cartoon channels with my five-year-old grandson. I was amazed as I listened to some of the big mysterious and unfamiliar words and names I heard. I attempted to pronounce one of the names, and my grandson was quick to correct me and pronounce it slowly so that I could mimic him. As I thought about this later, I realized how intelligent and teachable our children are. I thought about some of the more meaningful and comprehensive words in the Bible, such as *sanctification*, and I told myself, "I wonder if my five-year-old grandson Gabe can pronounce this word?" And sure enough, I challenged

Gabe to pronounce the word *sanctification*, and he did it beautifully. I then explained the meaning: when a person becomes good and obedient every day by loving God, obeying his parents, and studying the Bible stories. Now that may not be the exact interpretation as an adult may know it, but it's close enough for the child to understand in basic words. Ever since we have been practicing big words. It's been months since we started, and he remembers every one of them.

Once I popped that first word, *sanctification*, it became a cinch to think of other complicated and valuable words to teach my grandsons. You will be amazed at how quick to learn this young generation is. Don't miss this great opportunity for injecting their minds with spiritual and moral values from God's Word.

Many children are learning to say big words such as *supercalifragilisticexpialidocious*, even though they may not know the meaning. The roots of this word have been defined as follows: "super—'above,' cali—'beauty,' fragilistic—'delicate,' expiali—'to atone,' and docious—'educable.' According to the 1964 Walt Disney Film *Mary Poppins*, it is defined as "something to say when you have nothing to say."[1]

If our children can learn these big words, they can also learn the meaning and pronunciation of more complicated words from the Bible, such as:

- *Justification*—"God forgives me of all my sins, which Jesus paid for on the cross. I am holy (good) in God's eyes."

- *Praise and worship*—"When I tell the Lord Jesus that I love Him and I sing songs and psalms to glorify Him." Give examples.

- *Commandments*—"God's instructions to behave and succeed." Explain and help them memorize the Ten Commandments with illustrations and brief words.

- *Forgiveness*—"When we forgive someone for hurting us."

- *Resurrection*—"When Jesus died on the cross and became alive again."

- *Transformation*—"When we change our bad habits and obey God's Word."

- *Salvation*—"When we give our hearts to Jesus and turn away from evil."

Use the concordance in the back of the Bible for a new word adventure to train your child in the wisdom of God. The rewards will be eternal.

> My son, pay attention to what I say; listen closely to my words. Do not let them out of your sight, keep

them within your heart; for they are life to those who
find them and health to a man's whole body.

—PROVERBS 4:20–22

NIGHTMARES AND BAD DREAMS

Your child needs to know what to do when he has nightmares or
bad dreams. I taught my daughters and grandsons that whenever
they had a bad dream or fear came into their heart, they should
sing, "Jesus loves me, this I know; for the Bible tells me so…"

You can teach them to say, "In the name of Jesus, I will not be
afraid!" and "Jesus is my Lord."

But more importantly, we must become aware of the television
programming, video games, and all other forms of entertainment
available to children today. An enormous amount of children's TV
programs and electronic games are either overtly or subtly inun-
dated with witchcraft, magic, and spells. Today there seems to be
an obsession among our young people for everything that has to
do with vampires, wizards, zombies, and the occult.

Many parents become numb and passive, telling themselves
that as long as they go to church on Sunday, their children will
know the difference and will be all right. We rationalize that
the child is wise enough or old enough to know that what he is
watching is *not real* but fantasy.

This belief system is very erroneous. Young children become
conditioned at a very young age. They are gullible and believe
everything they see and hear. Even if you tell them, "Don't be
afraid; that spider is not real—it's a robot and will never harm

you," when the spirit of fear makes entry into the child's heart, nothing you say will make a difference. The child will always feel fear grip his heart and cause it to palpitate within every time he sees a spider, whether real or in a movie.

If a child has constant nightmares, I suggest you leave a tape recorder on all night in his room with praise and worship music at a very low volume. Praise music has a tremendous effect on the atmosphere. Evil spirits dislike praise and worship music.

Find out if there is anything evil your child plays with, such as toys or games, videos, movies, or music. Anything with demonic content has the ability to attract the influence of demons.

> In peace I will both lie down and sleep, for You, Lord,
> alone make me dwell in safety and confident trust.
> —PSALM 4:8, AMP

MENTAL DISORDERS

I recently read an article titled "In US, 1 in 5 Teens Have Serious Mental Disorder."[2] This article relates that, according to a startling new study, about one in five teens in the United States suffer from a mental disorder severe enough to impact their daily activities, either currently or at some point in their lives. The research also concludes that a higher percentage have or have had some sort of mental disorder, though less serious in nature.

> "The prevalence of severe emotional and behavior dis-
> orders is even higher than the most frequent major

physical conditions in adolescence, including asthma or diabetes, which have received widespread public health attention," the researchers write in the October issue of the *Journal of the American Academy of Child and Adolescent Psychiatry*.[3]

According to the researchers, this study, involving a nationally representative sample of 10,123 adolescents ages thirteen to eighteen in the continental United States, is the first to report the prevalence of a broad range of mental disorders. The mental disorders were assessed during interviews.

Anxiety disorders, such as panic disorders and social phobia, were the most common conditions (31.9 percent of teens had such a disorder), followed by behavior disorders, including attention-deficit/hyperactivity disorder or ADHD (19.1 percent), mood disorders, such as major depressive disorder (14.3 percent), and substance use disorders (11.4 percent).[4]

Our children are at risk. We must take action by getting serious about our walk with God and training our children to love and serve Him with all their hearts.

ESTABLISH AND DEVELOP A SOLID FOUNDATION FOR YOUR CHILD

This must be a hands-on experience. It has to be like putting together a puzzle that you refuse to give up on until the entire puzzle is knit together. A solid foundation consists of transparent love, discipline, and spiritual training. Unlike a fragile foundation constructed upon the sand, a solid, sturdy, reliable, and Word of God–based foundation will withstand and bear up to the storms and peer pressures of life.

Your child may stray, abandon the ship, and seem to be beyond hope, but you must know that if a foundation was solid and fixed from the beginning, it will withstand and endure sin, iniquity, drug addiction, peer pressure, witchcraft, false religions, and so many other things that this young generation is swayed and tempted with.

A solid and strong foundation is built upon the rock who is Jesus Christ. If you train your children from an early age, and you help them understand and believe that without Christ and the guidance of the Holy Spirit in their lives they are vulnerable to the attacks and destruction of the enemy, they will remain faithful. It is just a matter of time.

You must be tough and talk straight. You must say it out loud and with conviction and in love. If you're a Christian, make a decision to plant the seed of the Word of God into your child's heart. Be a role model of God's unconditional love. Pray powerful prayers. God is faithful to His Word!

*****

NOTES FOR CHAPTER THREE

1. Wikipedia.org, "Supercalifragilisticexpialidocious," http://en.wikipedia.org/wiki/Supercalifragilisticexpialidocious (accessed January 31, 2011).

2. MyHealthNewsDaily.com staff, "In US, 1 in 5 Teens Have Serious Mental Disorder," October 13, 2010, http://www.myhealthnewsdaily.com/children-mental-disorder-prevalence-101013-0550/ (accessed January 20, 2011).

3. Ibid.

4. Ibid.

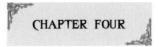
YOUR CHILDREN'S INHERITANCE

HOW TO FORM YOUR CHILDREN'S CHARACTER

Behold, children are a heritage from the Lord,
the fruit of the womb a reward.

—PSALM 127:3, AMP

THE BEST INHERITANCE that a father can leave to a son or daughter is an equal amount of love and discipline. Most parents have problems with their children's behavior. In order to have a sound foundation, the child needs to admire his parents and feel admired by them. Children also need to feel that they can trust and be friends with their parents. A healthy relationship forms the child's character positively. Children need to feel loved, appreciated, and admired by their parents in an environment that breeds consistent discipline and values. As children grow up, they perceive that their parents are heroes and will always satisfy their needs and protect them. These sentiments create part of their identities.

It is very sad to see that many parents are perceived as powerless and incapable of ruling their own lives. The child in these situations feels insecure and fearful. In an atmosphere of instability, ambiguity, and, many times, violence, the child learns to distrust and develop a character that doesn't allow him or her to deal properly with others.

Discipline is part of a child's healthy upbringing. Without discipline, there is chaos. However, there is wholesome discipline, and there is destructive discipline. Ask the Holy Spirit for help in this area.

I remember my childhood days when my brothers and sisters enjoyed playing games and chattering as normal children do. Yet the moment we heard our father's familiar knock on the door, we would all hurry to sit like little angels or the fury of my father would be unleashed like a storm. He was seeking respect, but what we experienced was tremendous fear.

However, change is possible. The person who wants to change and asks for God's help can receive miracles in his or her family. Take the first step today. Give your life and your family to God. God is willing to forgive and to restore all that Satan has stolen from you. Make the decision to change. Decide to forgive. Learn to love and to receive God's love. Start today to leave an inheritance of love and the fruit of the Spirit for your children.

CELEBRATE YOUR SON'S MASCULINITY

In the United States it is customary to have a special party for young girls when they reach their sixteenth birthday—*sweet sixteen*. In Latin American countries, families celebrate the *quinceañera* when the girl becomes fifteen years old. In a special ceremony, the daughter receives a blessing, symbolizing her transformation from an adolescent to a young woman. But how do we acknowledge and celebrate our boys' manhood? How do we support them? How do they know that they have become young men and need to conduct themselves like responsible young men?

When a Jewish boy becomes thirteen years old, his father honors him with a Bar Mitzvah celebration. This ritual suggests that the son has become of age and is obligated to observe the commandments. The young man makes a speech that traditionally begins with the phrase, "Today I am a man." The father recites a blessing, thanking God for removing the burden of being responsible for the son's sins. Now the child is old enough to be responsible for his own sins.

What about Americans? What do we do with our sons? For most of us, NOTHING!

The ages between thirteen and eighteen are very sensitive. When the son becomes eighteen, he feels liberated from his parents. When he reaches twenty-one, he considers himself an adult man. We must learn a lesson from the Jews. Christian parents must play a more important role in the lives of their children.

I do not have a son, but I believe that if I did, when he became thirteen years old, I would plan a celebration and have his father pray a blessing over him to indicate that at this age he continues to prepare himself to become a responsible young man. A young man who respects his parents, the law, and women will become a grown man who will honor God and his family.

I would also buy him a gold or silver ring or engraved cross as an initiation to a new stage in his life. We have a great responsibility as parents to guide our children in the fear and admonition of God's Word by modeling a lifestyle of love, respect, and commitment. My family had the great pleasure of celebrating our grandson's thirteenth birthday and putting this advice to work.

A single mother should seriously consider enrolling her son in a good church program that can teach and guide him during the difficult years of his life. Boys are at a much higher risk at this age than girls. We need to look for ways that will help us involve our sons in educational programs led by responsible Christian role models who will teach them how to live right.

Parents are the most important tutors that a son and daughter will ever have. What we model and live will be the school of experience that will guide their lives. *Celebrate your son's masculinity!* Give value and significance to the life of your son. Young adolescents can hardly wait to become thirteen. They feel as if a new freedom of lifestyle is on the horizon. If left fatherless and untrained, they can become rebellious and uncommitted.

Malachi 4:5–6 talks about a curse coming upon a whole nation if the fathers' hearts are not turned toward their children. Today we have a generation of hurting, defiant, and angry children who are not mature enough to process their anger.

Many men need to be set free from the curse of neglecting God's ordained roles. Many women need to be set free from irresponsible male domination. We need men who will take seriously the responsibility God has ordained for them.

It is a father's responsibility to leave an inheritance of moral stability and goodness (Prov. 13:22). One of the most important things we can do is to leave *a spiritual inheritance* for our children. It is our responsibility to influence the lives of our children with God's Word and His love for humanity.

When our children sense that we are willing to give our lives for them, never lie to them, and always want to do the best for them, they will begin to trust us. We leave them *an inheritance of trust.*

EMPOWER YOUR CHILDREN

Take a little time each day to pray and practice this advice. You will reap wonderful consequences. Train your children using God's precepts, and you will have a peaceful home.

Teach them to bless and keep promises.

Bless them in the morning and in the evening. Speak blessings over them and not curses. Our parents taught us to say, "God bless you." But nowadays we no longer give blessings. Teach your children to bless. It is biblical, and it causes the enemy to flee.

When we promise something to a child, we must do it. I

53

remember deep wounds, many of them caused by promises that never were fulfilled or explained.

Lead them to welcome Jesus into their hearts.

Teach your children at an early age to know God. When they are three, four, and five years old, lead them repeatedly in a prayer inviting Jesus into their hearts until they say, "Mom, I've already said that prayer."

Empower them to pray.

Teach your children the power of prayer. Give them examples of different prayers, such as prayers of thanksgiving, praise, healing, protection, and guidance. When my daughters were in grade school, they were taught a paraphrased scripture beginning with each letter of the alphabet. We repeated these scriptures in the form of prayers every day until they memorized them. Scripture memorization leaves a lasting impression in the heart of a child. Teach them to pray some of the Book of Psalms. It is not impossible. My mother taught me these prayers and psalms as a child, and I still remember them well.

Teach them how to know Satan.

Through cartoons on television, you can teach your child how Satan works. Use video games or a movie to describe the war between good and evil. Don't be afraid to talk about this subject. Children today are bombarded with violent entertainment portraying magic, violence, and witchcraft. If the secular world is not afraid to spend billions of dollars to seduce our children to spend hours each day in front of the TV and playing video games, then we too must take a stand to teach our children about the strategies of the enemy. Convey to them at an early age that the power of God is greater than the power of the enemy!

Teach them obedience.

Obedience can be learned. For a child to learn obedience and not fear his parents, it is important that we as parents are obedient to God and His Word. If this is not the case, we must begin by asking forgiveness from God and our children.

This book is for those who want to change and want to see their children spiritually healthy. Train your children by making sure they attend church, go to Bible studies, and get a good education, but also make sure they see you living out your faith on a daily basis. Set the biblical standard as to what is acceptable and not acceptable in the home. Even if you fail or let your guard down or disobey God, your children know you will go to God and ask His forgiveness. Your children will learn to be obedient because they see you are obedient to God.

Empower them to know the Holy Spirit.

I recommend that you pray about introducing the Holy Spirit to your child. I don't know where I would be today if it had not been for the help and direction of the Holy Spirit. The Bible says that the Holy Spirit is our friend, helper, comforter, teacher, advocate, and the one who teaches us and reveals the truth in the Scriptures.

As an abused child, I remember having many conversations

with the Holy Spirit. He always kept me in peace in the midst of the storms. Learn everything you can about the Holy Spirit, and teach your children to depend upon His help and guidance.

"Don't you know that you yourselves are God's temple and that God's Spirit lives in you?" (1 Cor. 3:16). As the temple of God, our spiritual being is inhabited by the Holy Spirit. Our inner being is where we stand up against the enemy.

Empower your child by applying sound correction.

One of the problems we face today is how to discipline our children. The law forbids using the *rod* as the Bible instructs us in several verses, including Proverbs 22:15: "Foolishness is bound up in the heart of a child; the rod of correction will drive it far from him" (NKJV).

What can we do? I have two daughters, and we only had to use the "rod" two times since they were very young. We used a ruler like they used in schools years ago. But my daughters never forgot about that experience. They only had to see the "rod," and they rapidly behaved.

Today, parents go to the school to argue with the teacher about their child's behavior, blaming the school for the problem. How absurd and counterproductive.

Ask for the Holy Spirit's help today in order to deal with your child's disciplinary problems. Never administer discipline in anger; wait until you calm down. Hug your child afterward. Be firm, fair, and caring. Don't be angry or cruel. Teach your child that you are the parent and you are in control. Don't discipline until you are under control.

It is a parent's responsibility to make sure his or her children are consistently and fairly disciplined. Even though they have a sin nature and are not naturally inclined to be good, if we rear them in a good environment and parent them correctly, giving them self-esteem and building them up, as they grow older they will make right choices. Don't wait until it is too late.

The apostle Paul says it this way in Romans 7:18: "I know that nothing good lives in me, that is, in my sinful nature." There will always be a war between our flesh and our spirit. God gives us the power to walk in the spirit and not the flesh.

Children need to learn that there are consequences for their behavior. Teach them that when they disobey God's Word and authority, there are consequences. Many children today have no self-control because no one has disciplined them. "He who spares the rod hates his son, but he who loves him is careful to discipline him" (Prov. 13:24).

All children flourish when they are loved, encouraged, and properly disciplined. Hug your children. Tickle them and wrestle with them. Smother them with kisses and funny words. It is necessary to continue praying and loving our children with all our hearts.

When they become older, we will not be able to discipline them, but yes, we can pray in faith, believing God's Word. Our words will perform wonders! Make sure you say lots of good words. The more good words you say, the better the atmosphere you create. This also works in marriages.

> A wholesome tongue is a tree of life.
> —Proverbs 15:4, nkjv

Keep your heart happy, and you will have happy children.

> He who is of a merry heart has a continual feast.
> —Proverbs 15:15, nkjv

Teach them how to work.

If we want confident and well-trained children, we have to teach them to work, starting at a very early age. A six-year-old child can make the bed, put away his shoes and toys, and organize his room. If my seven-year-old grandson can do it, so can yours. Today we have a lot of lazy children because their parents are lazy. The children imitate everything. It is never too late to train them.

Old folks can also learn new things. We must liberate our children from the curse of procrastination and laziness. Let's start early and demand order in the lives of our children, teaching them to do whatever is needed.

Teach them how to be positive.

There is a lot of information on this subject. To be positive is a habit that is shaped with practice. Our human nature wants to focus on all the negative things in life. It takes a lot of effort to create a habit of being positive. In order for our children to be positive in everything they do, we must be positive in everything that we do. Always find something positive to say about your pastor, relatives, friends, work, and home—in short, about everything you do. It is a speaking style that is learned and imitated. A negative person can never see goodness in another person or in that person's children or home. Teach your children to be positive in everything.

Teach them how to have joy.

"The joy of the Lord is [my] strength" (Neh. 8:10). A person who does not have joy is a sad person. How many people, even children, have you seen walking around with sad and angry faces? When a child sees his parents smiling and enjoying themselves, the child also learns how to smile and have a good time.

Joy is imitated. Joy is practiced. Smiling is something we do when we are happy. Christians always have a special reason to smile: Christ lives in us! Teach your children to feel and express joy and happiness in their lives. Start with yourself! Be an example.

Teach them how to praise God.

Praise and worship must be a part of our daily lives. Even if you don't know how to sing, always play sacred music in your home. Praises and sacred music drive away bad spirits from your home and mind. Teach your children the power of praise and worship to God.

Teach them how to defend themselves.

My six-year-old grandson already knows how to fend off somebody who tries to touch him sexually or tries to introduce him to witchcraft. These are subjects that you should discuss with your child at a very early age. The enemy knows the power of teaching and training a young child. Your goal should be to build a relationship so that your child can always confide in you when he faces trouble and difficulties.

When children are young, they perceive and believe everything. We must teach our children that we take care of our own bodies—they are not for any other person's use. My grandson has learned that when somebody tries to touch *his private parts*, he says no, runs, escapes from that person, goes to his mother, and tells her immediately without fear.

Regardless of what happens or happened, the child needs to be reassured that you will protect and defend him. You can prevent something serious from happening because your child has already been taught what to do if this situation arises. Many older boys and girls suffer today because of something traumatic that happened in their childhood and they didn't have the nerve and courage to tell their parents or anyone else.

In most situations of abuse, the victim is told not to tell anyone, or he or she will be in great danger. Fear paralyzes the victim. Teach your child that Satan works through people to cause evil to others.

Teach your child not to be afraid. Pray with him every night. Rebuke fear and the power of the enemy from entering your home.

Keep yourself pure so that the enemy will not have a stronghold in your family life.

We only have one opportunity to influence the lives of our children. Decide today that you will make your live count. Your children will thank you when they become older. Teach your children how to defend themselves and not be afraid of the enemy!

PARAPHRASED SCRIPTURE PRAYERS TAKEN FROM THE WOMEN OF DESTINY BIBLE[1]

Father, may my children be as the sons of Issachar and have understanding of the times (1 Chron. 12:32).

Lord, may my children seek You and Your strength. May they seek Your face forever (1 Chron. 16:11).

Lord, I pray that my children would set their heart and soul to seek You (1 Chron. 22:19).

Lord God, may my children stand every morning and every evening to give You thanks and praise (1 Chron. 23:30).

Lord, I pray that my children would delight in Your law and that they would meditate on it, pondering it day and night (Ps. 1:2).

Father, keep my children as the apple of Your eye; hide them under the shadow of Your wings (Ps. 17:8).

Show my children Your ways, O Lord; teach them Your paths. Lead them in Your truth and teach them, for You are the God of their salvation (Ps. 25:4–5).

Lord God, give my children understanding to know that You are their hiding place. You will preserve them from trouble and surround them with songs of deliverance (Ps. 32:7).

I pray, Father, that my children will delight themselves in You and that You would give them the desires of their heart (Ps. 37:4).

Create in my children a clean heart, O God, and renew a steadfast spirit within them (Ps. 51:10).

May my children trust in You with all their heart, and lean not on their own understanding. I pray that they will acknowledge You in all their ways and that You would direct their paths (Prov. 3:5–6).

I pray that my children would hear instruction and be wise, that they would not disdain it (Prov. 8:33).

Lord, may my children have pity on the poor, for they that have pity on the poor lend to You, and You will pay back what they have given (Prov. 19:17)

Lord, through wisdom may my children build their house, and by understanding may it be established. By knowledge may the rooms be filled with all precious and pleasant riches (Prov. 24:3–4).

O Lord, I pray that my children would understand that You are their salvation; may they trust in You and not be afraid. Be their strength and song; O God, become their salvation (Isa. 12:2).

COMMUNICATE LOVE AND COMMITMENT TO YOUR CHILDREN

Build up your children. Leave an inheritance of peace, joy, kindness, love, words of blessings, sound counsel, and admonition. Compliment them when they do something well done. Affirm them. Take time to say that you love them dearly.

Bless your children every day. Place your hand upon their heads and speak words of blessing. Enjoy the weekends, holidays, and vacations. Never go to bed angry with them.

Ask God to help you be a great mom and a great dad. Lighten up! Don't be so serious. Smile, laugh, sing, and goof off with your kids. Take them to the park and ball games. Act silly sometimes.

Speak God's Word over your children all the time. Begin by

speaking God's Word into your own life. The Word is like medicine: it heals (Prov. 4:20–22).

Every time you plan something with your family, think *inheritance* and make memories that will never be forgotten.

*****

NOTES FOR CHAPTER FOUR

1. Prayers are taken from the *Women of Destiny Bible* (Nashville: Thomas Nelson, 2000). Reprinted by permission. All rights reserved.

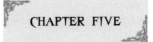
PREPARATION TO ENTER INTO THE ENEMY'S CAMP

BUILD UP YOUR FAITH

*For God did not give us a spirit of timidity (of cow-
ardice, of craven and cringing and fawning fear), but [He
has given us a spirit] of power and of love and of calm and
well-balanced mind and discipline and self-control.*

—2 TIMOTHY 1:7, AMP

YOU MUST BUILD up your faith through God's Word in prayer. Before you enter into the battle zone in prayer, make sure that your heart is right with God. Repent, and humble yourself. Renounce sin, confess all to God, and resist Satan in the name of Jesus. These steps are crucial if you want your prayers answered. You must be prepared, and you must be dressed in the full armor of God (Eph. 6:10–17), which is the

Word of God, Christ Jesus in us. This armor is necessary if you want your prayers and spiritual warfare to be effective.

The enemy will try to interrupt your thoughts as you pray and as you apply the necessary scriptures for your particular situation. The battleground will always be in your mind. This is the first area where the enemy will attack you. The mind is an important key in the battle against Satan. As you will remember, what a person thinks in his heart determines who he is and what he believes.

One place for spiritual warfare is in the prayer closet. Take all negative thoughts and imaginations and bring them captive to the obedience of Christ. When you do this, you will have peace in the midst of adversity. It is like pressing the *delete* button in order to erase something in your computer, or pressing the *eject* button on your CD player in order to remove a CD. The moment you resist the negative thoughts and confusion from your mind and bring your thoughts captive to the obedience of Christ by quoting the Word, the effect will be similar to ejecting a CD out of your player. It requires faith in God to cause biblical truths to be imprinted upon your mind and upon the minds of your family members. Spiritual warfare is something that must be engaged NOW! God's Word is alive and active NOW!

> We demolish arguments and every pretension that sets itself up against the knowledge of God, and we take captive every thought to make it obedient to Christ.
>
> —2 CORINTHIANS 10:5

When parents are willing to read, learn, and exercise the power of the Word of God to bring the thoughts in their minds into alignment with God's thoughts, then positive changes will happen.

Many times discouragement and anxiety will creep in as you press on toward the perfect will of God for your life and for the lives of your family. Resist them immediately. Do not become anxious. Your prayers and spiritual warfare are the *keys* that will foil and destroy the strategies of the enemy in the lives of your loved ones. Ask the Lord to open your spiritual eyes and understanding to see beyond the natural realm.

The Holy Spirit will be your teacher and your guide. You will learn to hear the voice of the Holy Spirit as you spend time praying and meditating in God's Word. Ask the Lord for discernment and for wisdom to understand when the enemy is attacking or when it is something that we are allowing. *God has given you power and authority over ALL the power of the enemy, and nothing shall harm you!*

DON'T STOP SERVING

Continue serving God and ministering to the needs of others. Use your God-given talents and abilities to rise above the negative circumstances. Wait upon the Lord, and expect to see your miracle unfold. Ignore negative comments from those who know you. Don't allow guilt, condemnation, and shame to rule in your life. Blaming yourself for your child's behavior is not going to stop the works of the devil in his life. Immediate action must be taken.

This must be action that focuses upon the love of God and upon your faith in the power of God's Word.

You might have been a victim yourself. Put everything behind you, and set your face like flint. Begin to trust the Lord and His Word. Don't be moved by what you can see, hear, know, or feel. Don't allow adverse circumstances to take up all of your prayer and supplication time. You must not allow the situation to consume your time, prayers, and fellowship with God. Continue serving, witnessing, teaching, praying, and doing all of those things that you were doing or have desired to do in your heart.

> "No weapon forged against you will prevail, and you will refute every tongue that accuses you. This is the heritage of the servants of the LORD, and this is their vindication from me," declares the LORD.
>
> —ISAIAH 54:17

Parents should not fear any single weapon devised by Satan against their loved ones. Remember that Satan is a defeated foe, and each and every demonic weapon is totally powerless in the face and power of Almighty God accessed by a Christian parent. The choice is up to you. Will you be defeated by fear, or will you be victorious in spiritual warfare because of your faith in Jesus Christ?

You might as well give up now if you are going to limit God by what you see, know, or hear. Get ready to see dramatic results if you can believe that the same resurrection power that raised

Christ from the dead dwells within you and that it is able to raise your loved one from spiritual death. Take your eyes off the clock, and allow God to have His way. As long as there is life, there is hope. A person who never gives up is a person who knows who he is, knows who God is, and knows how to access the power of God in warfare against demonic forces designed to cripple those who are weak and disoriented.

TESTIMONY OF ANSWERED PRAYER

It took my mother-in-law approximately fifteen years of intercession and prayers for three of her teenage sons to come back to the Lord after turning to lives of drug addiction. These boys were reared in a Christian home with a dad who was the pastor of the fastest-growing Spanish church in Brooklyn, New York. This praying and loving mom never gave up. When things seemed totally impossible, she increased in faith, love, and prayer. Her endurance paid off in miracles. Today, these grown men are involved in ministry and serving the Lord.

You must not give up! You must never quit!

Fathers, your children are more important than your friends and associates. Invest your love, time, and money in your children. It will be one of the greatest investments you will ever make in the lives and faith of your children.

There are records of people upon their deathbeds who were asked what were the most important things in life to them. Most of them declared that their relationship with their God and their relationship with their families were the most important things in life. All of their careers, accomplishments, and possessions were totally worthless at the end of life when compared to relationships.

A VERY IMPORTANT SECRET

Practice *God's love*. Nothing disperses the darkness, confusion, and the works of the enemy more effectively than walking in and practicing God's love. God is love, and He is motivated by love. As we dare to love our children and family unconditionally, the darkness has to depart from them eventually. Parents, your display of love in action in everything that you do will have a tremendous impact upon your family life.

I remember that both my husband and I found it difficult to demonstrate love and affection to our daughters when they were young. As we gained knowledge from reading and studying God's Word, we made a concentrated effort to be more affectionate and more loving in word and deed. My husband was reared in a home with four brothers and one sister. I had eight brothers and sisters in my family. Our families were neither affectionate nor demonstrative in their love. We played together and interacted but at a very shallow level.

My father-in-law was the pastor of a thriving church in New York. His first priority was his congregation. He had no quality time for his children. My father was a troubled man who was driven by evil spirits to abuse his family. My mother was very busy rearing nine children, and she was unable to stop to show much affection to any one of us in particular. Her free moments were dedicated to the church and prayer.

I am painting a picture that represents many families in America—always too busy or always too involved with the busy-ness of life, but never enough time for the things that count the most.

My husband and I were destined to continue passing on to our children the same lifestyle and patterns of behavior that we had experienced in our original families. In addition, the same attitudes, habits, and beliefs passed on to us could easily be passed on to our children. I call this living under the curse of ignorance.

But, praise God, we received knowledge while our children were still young. Today we are reaping the fruit of love, kindness, joy, and peace. We have a loving relationship with our children and grandchildren. It is a natural thing for my husband and me to hug, kiss, embrace, and say, "I love you," to each one of our daughters and grandchildren. It was not easy at first. We had to practice and practice. Like practicing piano lessons, the more we practice, the better it gets.

The same is true in our relationship with our heavenly Father. The more we practice entering into God's presence and fellowship with the Holy Spirit, the more intimate and familiar we become with Him. It becomes a relationship instead of a mere acquaintance. Learn to say, "Father, saturate my family with Your love. Cause Your love to permeate their beings and transform their lives."

PASSING JUDGMENT

We must be very careful not to pass judgment upon our children. God is the judge. Our flesh wants to predict and to dictate the verdict. We must be moved by faith in God's Word and not by our feelings and emotions.

Parents must learn to do as many things as they possibly can to encourage their children into becoming what God intended them to become. This includes:

- Loving them unconditionally

- Praying and interceding on their behalf

- Engaging in spiritual warfare against demonic forces coming against them

- Being a reflection of God's mercy and compassion

- Creating a peaceful environment at home

- Being a peacemaker

- Treating your children with as much respect as you would give to a guest

- Administering reasonable punishment as required

- Keeping your word and promises

+ Apologizing when you have wronged them

+ Controlling your temper and temper tantrums

+ Never screaming or yelling

+ Not doing or saying anything that you do not
  want your children to imitate

Learn to separate the sin from the child without condoning the sin. Always allow God's love to flow through you. There is sufficient cause for a child to continue in disobedience when parents continue to tell him that he is not good enough, he will never amount to anything, or he will never make it.

Reinforcing negative behavior only leads to more rebellion.

Remember that children are just that—they are children, not small adults. For example, if they accidentally spill a glass of milk, try to treat them in the same way that you would treat a visitor who spilled a glass of water. Your self-control can create incredible benefits for you and your family. It is worth the effort to thoughtfully teach and lovingly correct your children.

It is up to parents to control their own tempers, emotions, minds, and behavior. Parents must repent before God for their out-of-control emotions and behavior. It is important to ask the forgiveness of children who are still at home or children who are away from home who have endured out-of-control emotions or behaviors of the parents.

It is important for children to know that their parents are

taking a stand in order to please the Lord in all things. Children need to know that their parents love them and that they are praying for them. It is important to leave the past behind and to create a positive future. God is able to heal any hurt, no matter how devastating the wounds or how deep the scars.

As God restores each person to wholeness, it is easier to embrace each new day. Your children will learn that God is real when they see how much you trust God, how well you serve Him, and how much your behavior has changed toward loving each one of them as unique gifts from God.

GUILT AND CONDEMNATION

A very delicate area in which I see many parents fall is the overwhelming feelings of guilt and condemnation for the sins of their children.

You must remember that Satan is the deceiver and the father of all lies. Sin originated with Satan. The enemy will lie to you, telling you that it is your fault because of your past sins and mistakes. This is a lie of the enemy that you absolutely must not believe.

Reverse the curse of the enemy, and refuse to continue living under guilt and condemnation. Speak life from now on. The enemy wants to steal your faith; that is his ultimate goal. He could care less about everything that you do and how religious you are. He's just interested in robbing you of your faith in Jesus Christ. *Do not let guilt rob you of truth.*

Faith is believing that God can and will do what He promises.

Take hold of God's precious promises, stand firm, and learn to resist Satan. Speak the Word. Chew and digest the Word. Pray the Word. Believe and trust God's Word for you and for all of your family. Nothing else will help. God is ready to restore everything the enemy has taken from you! Make a decision to serve Him with all your heart.

> Therefore, there is now no condemnation for those who are in Christ Jesus.
>
> —ROMANS 8:1

ONLY IN GOD'S PRESENCE

In my husband's presence I am able to find understanding and companionship. In the presence of my pastor I am able to receive encouragement and prayer. Many people are able to go to a psychiatrist, and they learn to cope with their problems. When they go to their physician, he will diagnose and prescribe medication to help them. If they go to their employer, they will receive training, new skills, and compensation. They also may go to their therapist, and he will give them help for one more day. In a mother's presence, usually you will find nurturing and attention. In a friend's presence, you'll find support and a listening ear.

But only when you enter into the presence of God will you be able to find and receive healing and restoration for your spirit, soul, and body. Not only that, but you will also find direction, communion, the guidance of the Holy Spirit, understanding and wisdom, provision, forgiveness, and power over all the works of the enemy. We can fill up several pages of the many wonderful things we can receive in God's presence.

I also find it very interesting when I find correction in His presence. The Lord will uncover the idols hidden in our lives as we proceed to enter and tarry in His presence. He also reveals unconfessed sins.

As we learn to walk in obedience, all of the old junk and excess baggage that we carry in our souls begins to come out, and they are replaced with God's love and the fruit of the Spirit.

How awesome to be able to trust the Lord completely and to surrender our lives and our family totally to His care. Only in God's presence are the battles won!

What you put into your heart will come out of your mouth. If you put guilt and negative thoughts into your mind, then they will come out of your mouth as a curse upon your family. If you put love, mercy, and grace into your heart, then love, mercy, and grace will come out of your mouth to bless your family. The choice is yours.

David said to the Philistine Goliath, "All those gathered here will know that it is not by sword or spear that the LORD saves; for the battle is the LORD's, and he will give all of you into our hands" (1 Sam. 17:47).

Can you imagine a boy brave enough to fight a Philistine giant who was greatly feared by the Israelite army? What was it that gave a young shepherd the courage to wage war against a Philistine giant? It was his faith in God and his faith that God would deliver the enemy into his hand. The reason that David had this type of faith is because he spent time in God's presence.

In His presence you will find peace, and in His Word you will find instruction for every need in your life. You don't have to spend the rest of your life coping and trying to make things work by yourself. Healing and deliverance are for you and all your family! God is able to do the impossible!

WARNING

The battleground against Satan will be in your mind. Your thoughts will carry on conversations. You will say things in your mind that you will learn not to say with your mouth. For example: "It's no use; my children will never amount to anything." Discipline yourself to bring those thoughts captive to the obedience of Christ as you confess God's Word over them. It is God who helps your children become the people that He intended them to become.

One important place of spiritual warfare is in prayer. This is the place where the victories are won. Make prayer a habit. Whenever the enemy tries to attack your mind with wrong attitudes, discouragement, guilt, condemnation, anger, confusion, panic attacks, or any other negative thought, immediately begin to pray the Word and to declare your position in Christ. You are a child of God, and the evil one cannot harm you. You are a joint-heir with Christ and more than a conqueror. You are "in Christ," and Christ victoriously defeated Satan in the past, now, and for all eternity.

When strife enters your home through your child or loved one, immediately pray and bring down the strongholds with the Word of God. Don't wait until after you have joined in the strife. Refuse to be a part of it. Allow God's love to rule your heart, and speak words of peace and life.

Discipline your mind and your tongue. Memorize at least one scripture a week, and teach it to your children. Make regular deposits of scriptures into your heart and mind, and the Holy Spirit will be able to make withdrawals for you when you need them the most. Refuse to allow your tongue to speak death. Always speak life—even when your flesh and your mind demand to stand up for your rights, and even when you know you are right. Build up instead of tear down. Encourage instead of discourage.

There is power in your tongue to give life or to destroy, to cause anger or to bring peace, and to bring unity or cause division. There is power in God's love! Go against your flesh and speak life. Command your flesh to walk in love. Love will disperse the darkness. If you have ever experienced the overwhelming, unconditional love of God, then you should be willing to allow God to love your children unconditionally through the power of your tongue. Unconditional love is an enormously powerful instrument that can be used to encourage your children or to destroy their hopes and dreams. It is your choice. You can build up or you can diminish. Since God chooses to build you up with the truth of His Word, then you should choose to build up your children with your words.

> The tongue has the power of life and death, and those who love it will eat its fruit.
>
> —PROVERBS 18:21

> You will also declare a thing, and it will be established
> for you; so light will shine on your ways.
>
> —Job 22:28, nkjv

The word *declare* means to proclaim, decree, and to pronounce. The word *established* means instituted, fixed, proved, and permanent.

Whatever we decide or say with our tongue will be fixed and will be permanent. We have *dynamic power in our mouths*—to lift up or tear down, to heal or to kill! *We choose our words and thoughts!*

In the Midst of the Storm

As you enter into spiritual warfare prayer, do not be moved by the increased negative behavior of your child or loved one. Do not be moved by the lies and arguments, how your child looks at you, or by what he or she does.

Your child is not happy separated from God. Intensify your prayers, and demonstrate your love when things seem to get worse. Submit your child to God. This is not something you can do with your own strength and strategies. Your dependence and control will only bring disappointment and failure. *There must be a complete surrendering to God of all your cares and concerns.* Only then will God be able to act on your behalf to perform His Word.

It is not a simple matter to surrender our child or loved one to God. It is not easy to say, "God, he's Yours. Do whatever it takes to save him!" The thoughts of feeling guilt and condemnation if something bad happens to them will stop many people from praying this prayer.

To keep your mind in perspective, you must try to remember that God is a just God. His ways are not our ways. The bottom line is that God answers the fervent prayers of a righteous man or woman.

Keep calm and receive God's peace, especially when the storm is raging in intensity. Nothing confuses the enemy more than a child of God who is not moved by the tactics and strategies of the enemy.

Believe that God will save your children. It may be quickly, or it may take many years, as it did for my brothers-in-law. But always remember that their eternal salvation is at stake. Don't give up. Time is very short, and our journey on this earth will soon be over. Keep on believing in God, and do not let the element of fear and stress become a hindrance. Jesus is the burden bearer and the yoke breaker, and His anointing in your life will cause every demon to bow down to the name of Jesus. If you carry the burdens, then Jesus cannot. Be at peace, dear parent. *You are going to see in these last days a great outpouring of His Spirit upon all flesh.*

It took me a long time to learn to walk in peace over the different situations that arose in my children's lives. I wanted to help God make the changes. It only made me miserable and stressed out. My entire prayer life was concentrated around the concerns that I had over my children.

One day I surrendered. The effect and result of my total surrender to God and my trust in His Word are making a tremendous impact in the lives of my children and family. It is only when we, as parents, surrender our own will and the lives of our loved ones to God that He will begin to create a new family that begins to walk in the law of love.

God has promised to keep us and to strengthen us in the midst of the storms. *Please don't ever underestimate the power of God within you to deliver you and your loved ones out of the hand of the enemy.* The Lord has promised in His Word to save our lost children. He will keep His promises to those who love Him with all of their hearts and who keep His commandments. Continue declaring and pronouncing the Word of God over your children, and you will see it performed in many miraculous ways in this life.

Every day I have learned to ask God to impart upon me and my husband wisdom and understanding. I cannot adequately express the changes taking place in our family life and ministry because of these two great attributes being imparted upon us by the Holy Spirit. The Word says to ask, and it shall be given unto you. When we ask for wisdom and understanding, it is given to us for the purpose of loving our family and ministering to others.

> If any of you lacks wisdom, he should ask God, who gives generously to all without finding fault, and it will be given to him.
>
> —James 1:5

> Get wisdom! Get understanding! Do not forget, nor
> turn away from the words of my mouth.... Wisdom is
> the principal thing.
>
> —PROVERBS 4:5, 7, NKJV

Intellectual knowledge alone does not automatically provide wisdom and understanding. It takes more than intellectual knowledge. It takes wisdom and understanding of intellectual principles learned so that they can be applied effectively to daily life. This is also true for spiritual knowledge. It takes wisdom and understanding of spiritual principles learned so that they can be applied effectively in spiritual warfare.

Few of us really believe in our hearts that prayer is where the action is. Many believe that intelligence, logic, and reasoning can accomplish all things. All of these things may be profitable and accomplish much success, but in the warfare against evil spirits, only one thing is effective—the supernatural power of the Holy Spirit at work within us and released only by our believing prayer and our faith in God.

TRAINING MIGHTY LITTLE WARRIORS

I firmly recommend to all parents with young children that they begin early training your children how to pray spiritual warfare prayers. Let them become aware of who their enemy is. Don't keep your children ignorant about their number one enemy. They are capable of fully understanding good and evil when they watch cartoons and children's programs on TV. Why not understand the real supernatural world in which they live? Don't wait until they learn to fear the devil and demons, especially in their dreams. They already know all about violence and self-defense. Teach them who is the author of violence, death, lies, hate, and evil. *God has created within their spirits the capacity to understand the things of the supernatural and spiritual world.*

Your children can become *mighty little warriors* who are not afraid and who can pray instantaneously when danger comes to them. They learn very fast, but you must program and instill in them everything that pertains to how godliness overcomes evil. Place as much importance in training them in spiritual warfare as you do in teaching them the ABCs.

In the midst of storms, God's power within us is always greater. Your children can learn to pray in the middle of the night when evil spirits come to scare them with nightmares. Instead of screaming for help, they can learn to plead the blood of Jesus and see the results firsthand themselves. It is the responsibility of parents to train their children to stay away from evil things that can enter into their minds and spirits. Evil spirits can harass and torment children and affect their behavior. We must consistently pray and plead the blood of Jesus over our family. There is power in the blood of Jesus!

> And they have overcome (conquered) him by means of the blood of the Lamb and by the utterance of their testimony.
>
> —Revelation 12:11, amp

A child is affected not only by what he sees and hears but also by what surrounds him. Parents may think they are watching X-rated movies in a private room away from the children, but these same X-rated spirits will affect the behavior and sleep patterns of the children. They don't even have to be in the same room. Everything both good and bad in the spiritual realm gets transferred through the parents to the children, up to the fourth generation (Exod. 20:5). We must set an example before our children that will prepare them for eternal life.

The good news is that even if only one of the parents is serving God and walking in obedience, he or she has the power and authority to stand in the gap for the children and to plead the blood of Jesus for cleansing and protection. Also, you can ask God to place a hedge of protection from evil around your children (Job 1:10). Don't ever underestimate the power of God in you against all of the strongholds of the enemy. *You can be living in a hellhole and still live in peace.* As you continue resisting evil, you will see victories won one after another. God is able to deliver your children out of the hand of the enemy.

> But this is what the LORD says: "Yes, captives will be taken from warriors, and plunder retrieved from the fierce; I will contend with those who contend with you, and your children I will save.
>
> —ISAIAH 49:25

This should encourage parents when they clearly understand that God Himself contends with evil spirits who seek to affect the peace and stability of our children.

God often uses our faith in Jesus Christ and our prayers based on Scripture so that our rebellious children will be saved. *Don't give up! Persevere!* God's power is the only effective weapon against Satan and the demonic forces that try to keep our children from genuine reconciliation with God and eternal life. Parents, you have dynamic keys! Keep on believing and praying for your children.

BINDING AND LOOSING—LEARN TO USE THE KEYS OF THE KINGDOM

Jesus said we have power over all of the power of the enemy. When He gave us the keys of binding and loosing, He also gave us the authority to use them. Keys are to open and to lock up something. The Bible uses the word *keys* to describe the action of binding something and loosing something. Keys in the Bible refer to the delegated authority given to believers. Be ready to see dramatic changes as you use these spiritual keys.

> I will give you the keys of the kingdom of heaven; whatever you bind on earth will be bound in heaven, and whatever you loose on earth will be loosed in heaven.
>
> —MATTHEW 16:19

> I have given you authority to trample on snakes and
> scorpions and to overcome *all* the power of the enemy;
> nothing will harm you.
>
> —LUKE 10:19, EMPHASIS ADDED

Satan is ferociously determined to destroy you and your family. He doesn't care about your child's willpower. He works without ceasing to break that willpower. Therefore you must also pray and determine without ceasing that Satan will not control the will of your child. Satan does not consider your child's will! In fact, Satan tries to diminish the godly power of your child's will against demonic forces.

> And that they will come to their senses and escape
> from the trap of the devil, who has taken them captive
> to do his will.
>
> —2 TIMOTHY 2:26

We can pray against the negative will of our children by bombarding the forces of hell with spiritual warfare and by trusting God and His Word as we stand firm in our confession. *We must determine not to give up as we continue loving the person and hating the sin.* Our godly example and actions under all circumstances will have a lasting impression upon our children. The secret is in your belief that God's power within you is greater than the power of the enemy.

Using the keys of binding and loosing will have a tremendous impact upon your prayers and spiritual warfare. Bind every evil spirit that you know is controlling your loved one, and loose a good spirit, according to the Word of God.

For example, bind the spirits of loneliness, restlessness, and rejection. These are some of the most persistent and prevalent spirits to attach themselves to teenagers by attracting them to ungodly friends and influences. Pray that God will send godly friends and influences into your child's life. Loose the spirit of love, peace, joy, and a sound mind. Bind the evil spirits of lies and deception, disobedience, fear, and torment of the enemy; loose the spirit of truth and understanding and of peace and God's love.

As a born-again believer who is filled with the Holy Spirit, you are equipped to go into battle for your children and family. Our weapons are not of the flesh. The Bible says they are "mighty in God for pulling down strongholds" (2 Cor. 10:4, NKJV). Use your keys and your spiritual weapons: the name of Jesus, the blood of Jesus, the power of the Holy Spirit, praise and worship, the prayer of agreement, and the Word of God. When you put into action your spiritual weapons against satanic forces, you will see the walls of deception and the strongholds of the enemy destroyed in the lives of your loved ones.

You have every right to fight for your possessions. Children are your possessions, given to you by God, and Satan will try to trespass against and steal them. Rebuke the spirit of fear and strengthen your inner man with truth. Take up your shield of faith and the sword of the Spirit (the Bible), and you will be amazed at what God will do through your trust and confidence in

His Word. Remember, it is not your power or your strength but God's Spirit at work through you.

> "Not by might nor by power, but by my Spirit," says the LORD Almighty.
>
> —ZECHARIAH 4:6

> Sons are a heritage from the LORD, children a reward from him.
>
> —PSALM 127:3

THE DESTRUCTIVE EFFECTS OF LUST AND PORNOGRAPHY

Several years ago I read a striking headline that reflected the morals of our nation. It said, "Sex sailing into mainstream TV, films full steam ahead. As barriers fall, many wonder: What's next?"

Have you wondered why so many marriages break up because of sexual sins such as adultery, infidelity, and addictions to pornography? There is also incest, molestation, sexual abuse, jealousy, arguments, and affairs. Immorality is rampant, even in many so-called Christian homes. The more I counsel with married couples and single women, the more convinced I am that Satan has a plan for the destruction of all families. Surveys reveal that divorce in out of control in both secular and Christian families.

It all began with the fall of man. The Bible refers to the sins of the parents visiting the family up to the fourth generation.

In my grandparents' families there was witchcraft, sexual abuse, addictions, idol worship, and many other things. I have been able to observe how different family members have been affected by the same patterns of abuse and addiction as their parents were affected.

The transference of these spirits continues from generation to generation until a child of God with knowledge of the Word and of his legal rights takes up his rightful position and breaks the power of strongholds over his family. In my case, I was a victim of abuse.

I remember when my first daughter was born. I became extremely impatient when she cried all night and slept all day. In my impatience I would shake the crib and grind my teeth as her little body shook in the crib. Only by the grace of God did I manage to control myself. The same spirit of abuse wanted to take control of me and turn me into an abuser of my children.

That was my destiny, if Satan had had his way. But, praise the Lord, it was precisely during that time that I went to a women's meeting where I was able to receive instruction from a woman who knew the Word of God. The truth of God's Word set me free from the curse of abuse. After that I was able to take my little daughter in my arms and sing "Jesus Loves You" as I gently prayed for God to give me wisdom to train my daughter to become a woman of God. My life was never the same after that experience.

The abuse that I suffered left me with many consequences that affected my life for many years. The result of sexual abuse in any degree can create many bad habits and altered thought patterns in the victim. Immorality in marriage can be traced to some form of abuse, sexual or otherwise. In a home where abuse is practiced, the entire family suffers even if each member is not a direct victim of the abuse. The same spirits affect all of the members of that family.

Many wife abusers will tell you that their father abused their mothers. Many prostitutes will tell you that some family member sexually abused them. Many unfaithful wives will tell you that their father abused them. Many fathers who cannot get along with their daughters or sons will tell you that they did not have a good relationship with their father or mother. Many husbands who do not respect their wives will tell you that their father did not respect their mothers. Many homosexual men will tell you that they were molested by a family member or another man when they were very young. The cycle continues, and it is very vicious.

Lust and pornography will destroy marriages and relationships. The root has to be destroyed, and the person's mind has to be renewed by the Word of God and by fellowship with the Holy Spirit. These sins are never committed alone. Satan is always a participant, and your children and their children are the inheritors of the same sin or sins.

We are constantly being bombarded by sexually explicit images through the airways and all kinds of media and electronic devices. Our cell phones, computers, TV, video games, the Facebook phenomenon, and texting are impacting our lives in many ways. All these forms of connecting and forming relationships have also opened the door for easy escapism into the readily available world of lust and pornography. Even our adolescents are being affected and influenced by this rage.

Recently I did a study of forty pastors and their wives. I asked them to write a five-page autobiography of their family of origin and tell how their experiences affected their own lives and marriages. The results were incredible. Every one of them had been a victim of some past iniquity of their parents. Every one of them had been a target of Satan for destruction and failure. Every one of them was able to testify that they were able to overcome by the blood of the Lamb and the word of their testimony. Praise God! Some were still struggling, but all knew the source of their struggle.

Ignorance will keep a person bound and ignorant. We, as Christians who have the truth at our disposal, must learn what the Word of God says about us and the provisions already made available for a victorious life. We cannot remain ignorant any longer. We must engage in spiritual warfare and fervent prayers for our loved ones and stop the disintegration of our families. I challenge you to step out of the realm of ignorance and into the wonderful realm of God's wisdom and understanding.

> Then you will know the truth, and the truth will set you free.
>
> —John 8:32

> It is for freedom that Christ has set us free. Stand firm, then, and do not let yourselves be burdened again by a yoke of slavery.
>
> —GALATIANS 5:1

You are the most influential person on this earth who can stand in the gap for your children or loved ones to bring them back to God!

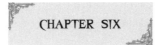

CHAPTER SIX

PRAYING FOR YOUR CHILDREN

SCRIPTURE SUPPORT FOR PRAYERS FOR SPIRITUAL
GROWTH

*Truly I tell you, whoever says to this mountain, Be lifted
up and thrown into the sea! and does not doubt at all in his
heart but believes that what he says will take place, it will
be done for him. For this reason I am telling you, whatever you ask for in prayer, believe (trust and be confident) that it is granted to you, and you will [get it].*

—MARK 11:23–24, AMP

LEARN TO SCRIPTURE-PRAY even from the time your children are in the womb. Continue adding scriptures as the
Holy Spirit gives them to you. The following scriptures
have been selected for your guidance as you pray for your children.

KNOWLEDGE OF JESUS AT AN EARLY AGE

*Father, draw them to Jesus Christ from an early age
and cause them to seek Him.*

Josiah was eight years....He did what was right in
the eyes of the LORD....While he was still young, he
began to seek the God of his father David.

—2 CHRONICLES 34:1–3

O God, you are my God, earnestly I seek you; my
soul thirsts for you, my body longs for you, in a
dry and weary land where there is no water.

—PSALM 63:1

HATRED OF SIN

Lord, place in them a hatred for sin.

Let those who love the LORD hate evil, for he guards
the lives of his faithful ones and delivers them from
the hand of the wicked.

—PSALM 97:10

PROTECTION FROM THE ENEMY

Lord, protect them from the enemy.

My prayer is not that you take them out of the world but that you protect them from the evil one.

—JOHN 17:15

RESPECT FOR AUTHORITY

Help them to respect those who have authority.

Everyone must submit himself to the governing authorities, for there is no authority except that which God has established. The authorities that exist have been established by God.

—ROMANS 13:1

HEALTHY RELATIONSHIPS

Father, lead them to healthy friendships, and protect them from the wrong ones.

My son, if sinners entice you, do not give in to them. If they say, "Come along with us…" My son, do not go along with them, do not set foot on their paths.

—PROVERBS 1:10–11, 15

A RESPONSIBLE, EXCELLENT SPIRIT

Lord, help them to be responsible in all of their relationships. Place in them an excellent spirit.

Now Daniel so distinguished himself among the administrators and the satraps by his exceptional qualities that the king planned to set him over the whole kingdom.

—DANIEL 6:3

SUBMISSION TO GOD

Lord, help them to completely submit themselves to You and to resist Satan.

Submit yourselves, then, to God. Resist the devil, and he will flee from you.

—JAMES 4:7

GOD'S CHOICE FOR A SPOUSE

Protect them, Lord, from the wrong companion, and help them to wait for the companion You have predestined for them.

Do not be yoked together with unbelievers. For what do righteousness and wickedness have in common? Or what fellowship can light have with darkness? What harmony is there between Christ and Belial? What does a believer have in common with an unbeliever? What agreement is there between the temple of God and idols? For we are the temple of the living God. As God has said: "I will live with them and walk among them, and I will be their God, and they will be my people."

"Therefore, come out from them and be separate, says the Lord. Touch no unclean thing, and I will receive you."

—2 CORINTHIANS 6:14–17

SEXUAL PURITY

Father, help them, as well as their future spouse, to stay pure until marriage.

Flee from sexual immorality. All other sins a man commits are outside his body, but he who sins sexually sins against his own body. Do you not know that your body is a temple of the Holy Spirit, who is in you, whom you have received from God? You are not your own; you were bought at a price. Therefore honor God with your body.

—1 CORINTHIANS 6:18–20

HEDGE OF PROTECTION

Lord, place a hedge of protection around them so that no evil will befall them.

Therefore I will block her path with thornbushes; I will wall her in so that she cannot find her way.

—HOSEA 2:6

It is God who arms me with strength and makes my way perfect.

—2 SAMUEL 22:33

ANGELIC PROTECTION

Thank You, Father, for Your angels that protect and keep them.

For he will command his angels concerning you to guard you in all your ways; they will lift you up in their hands, so that you will not strike your foot against a stone.

—PSALM 91:11–12

GROWTH IN WISDOM

Lord, cause them to grow in wisdom.

And Jesus grew in wisdom and stature, and in favor with God and men.

—LUKE 2:52

PROTECTION FROM PESTILENCE AND DESTRUCTION

Protect my children and loved ones from all pestilence and destruction.

Surely he will save you from the fowler's snare and from the deadly pestilence.

—PSALM 91:3

PROTECTION FROM WEAPONS FORMED AGAINST THEM

Father, protect them from every weapon formed against them.

"No weapon forged against you will prevail, and you will refute every tongue that accuses you. This is the heritage of the servants of the LORD, and this is their vindication from me," declares the LORD.

—ISAIAH 54:17

WISDOM AND UNDERSTANDING

Lord, teach them to apply their hearts unto wisdom and understanding.

Teach us to number our days aright, that we may gain a heart of wisdom.

—PSALM 90:12

But Daniel resolved not to defile himself with the royal food and wine, and he asked the chief official for permission not to defile himself this way.

—DANIEL 1:8

STRONG IN SPIRIT

Father, help my children grow strong in spirit and wisdom. May Your grace be upon them.

And the child grew and became strong; he was filled with wisdom, and the grace of God was upon him.

—LUKE 2:40

Keeping of God's Commandments

Cause their hearts to keep Your commandments.

Let love and faithfulness never leave you; bind them around your neck, write them on the tablet of your heart.

—Proverbs 3:3

To Honor the Lord

Father, I pray that my children will honor the Lord with all their substance.

Honor the Lord with your wealth, with the firstfruits of all your crops.

—Proverbs 3:9

True Worshipers

Father, cause them to become true worshipers who will worship You in Spirit and truth.

Yet a time is coming and has now come when the true worshipers will worship the Father in spirit and truth, for they are the kind of worshipers the Father seeks.

—John 4:23

KNOWLEDGE FROM THE WORD

Father God, help my children gain knowledge from Your Word so they will live and prosper.

My people are destroyed from lack of knowledge.
—HOSEA 4:6

CHAPTER SEVEN

BRINGING DOWN STRONGHOLDS

DEFEATING THE WORKS OF THE ENEMY

The reason the Son of God appeared was to destroy the devil's work.
—1 JOHN 3:8

THIS CHAPTER IS for victimized children and adults of abuse, rape, incest, neglect, and abandonment, as well as for children with attention disorders. The hidden secrets of sexual and physical abuse have been one of the most binding and shameful things that countless millions of men, women, and children are trying to cope with every day of their lives.

I am here to tell you that you don't have to continue living with the shame, guilt, hatred, memories, anger, and the feelings and lies of the enemy any longer. I was there—for many years of my life. I was a prisoner and a slave, controlled by my thoughts and emotions. I was a slave to the spirits of hatred, abuse, and perversion.

I was just an innocent six-year-old girl who trusted her daddy and became his victim. But today I am set free, and you can be too!

I will now take you on a mini-excursion of the battle between good and evil. I have every intention of exposing the devil's strategies through abuse and of helping you to become free.

THE HIDDEN SECRETS

The reason so many still live with the secrets is because they were taught and instructed not to tell anyone, or there would be very real and harsh consequences. As people mature to the age of understanding and accountability, they still keep the secrets for fear of being misunderstood and judged. Not only that, but the enemy of their souls will make them think that no one will believe them and that somehow they could have prevented the abuse. Many times during counseling with victims of abuse, I have heard that the feeling of guilt keeps coming back because they remember times when they enjoyed the abuse and perversion. Sex was created for procreation and pleasure within the marriage covenant. It is Satan who perverts everything and causes people's minds to be subjugated to the bondage of sin and slavery.

For many victims, these experiences have resulted in broken marriages, resentments, hatred, unforgiveness, lack of commitment, suspicion, low self-esteem, severe attacks from the enemy, promiscuity, homosexuality, lesbianism, masturbation, confusion, lack of friends, bad relationships, procrastination, bad eating habits, insatiable desires, addictions, mistrust, nervous breakdowns, pornography, and blaming God—among many others.

Yet I will repeat again that some people may find help going to a professional counselor or doctor, and some may find help talking about it with friends, relatives, or a trusted parent. Some may even find help talking to a pastor or priest. But I firmly believe that *only* in the presence of God Almighty, your heavenly Father, will you find healing and cleansing!

To reach the point of healing, a person first needs understanding and instruction. You can start by asking the Holy Spirit to help you. He is your best teacher and friend. I recommend that you seek the advice of a mature Christian man (for males) or woman (for females) in your church whose life is an example of godliness and compassion.

For the men, I also recommend you seek out a mature and godly Christian couple or a Christian counselor or pastor who can help you understand the root of the problems in your life.

Keep in mind that we wrestle not against flesh and blood. It is not the person who abuses whom we must come against, but it is the enemy of our soul who influences the person. The thoughts of condemnation must be brought captive to the obedience of Christ. *Once we surrender our lives to God, we become new creations or new daughters and sons in Christ Jesus.* The past is blotted out by the blood of Jesus Christ. Now we have to think differently. Our minds must be renewed each day by the Word. The awesome power in the Word of God pushes out the junk in a Christian's life and replaces it with the fruit of the Spirit.

> But the fruit of the Spirit is love, joy, peace, patience, kindness, goodness, faithfulness, gentleness and self-control.
>
> —GALATIANS 5:22–23

You must make a quality decision to allow your heavenly Father, through Christ Jesus and the work of the Holy Spirit, to make you whole again. Nothing works better than applying one of God's principles from the Word each day. Go against your negative feelings. Take control of your body and your thoughts. You are in warfare. There's a battle for your faith going on. You can be whole again. You are special and unique. *You were created with a purpose.* Jesus loves you with an unconditional love. He gave His life for you!

If a victim of abuse does not get the necessary help and continues merely *coping* with the problems, the results will be detrimental. The same pattern of behavior will be imitated by the children. The Bible says that the sins of the parents visit (get transferred) to the children to the fourth generation. It is time that we who believe in the redeeming work of Calvary and the triumphant victory that Jesus wrought for us take action to stop and break the influence of the sins of our parents visiting us to the fourth generation. We have been redeemed from the curse of the law, but we must declare our position in Christ and appropriate God's promises. Abuse victims must move on from *coping* to *healing.*

Many Christians do not know that they have been redeemed and set free from the curse of the law. Satan knows that they are ignorant, and he continues to visit them with all of the sins of their parents, such as abuse, alcoholism, addictions, sickness, diseases, negative thought patterns, lust, rebellion, poverty, and divorce.

Stand up, mighty warrior; resist the enemy, and he will flee from you. Drive him out of your life and the lives of your children. Start putting off the things of the stinking old man, and begin dressing yourself with the robes of royalty that have been designated and are waiting for you. We are daughters and sons of royalty, and we have been given authority to rule and to reign over all of the works of the enemy—past and present.

> You are worthy to take the scroll and to open its seals, because you were slain, and with your blood you purchased men for God from every tribe and language and people and nation. You have made them to be a kingdom and priests to serve our God, and they will reign on the earth.
>
> —Revelation 5:9–10

Children develop problems because of many reasons. Sometimes they are victims. Other times they willfully disobey authority and as a result suffer many consequences from the hand of the enemy. Some children learn to imitate their parents. Others are born with inherited negative characteristics and sinful habits. Many children suffer from attention disorders, which I also believe is a stronghold of the enemy that can be destroyed. Ultimately, the enemy of our souls plays a big role in the lives of children.

It is time for all Christian parents to play the greatest role of direct intervention to all demonic activity in the lives of their children and loved ones. We perish for lack of knowledge, but *once that knowledge is received and applied, everything can change*!

> My people are destroyed from lack of knowledge. Because you have rejected knowledge, I also reject you as my priests; because you have ignored the law of your God, I also will ignore your children.
>
> —HOSEA 4:6

DEMONIC ATTACKS

An alarmingly high percentage of our children are under demonic attacks. Children are hitting, kicking, yelling, and cursing at their parents. Many children of Christian parents have become blatantly disobedient. (The percentage is much higher in non-Christian homes.) I have counseled with desperate mothers who tell me that even spanking and strict restrictions do not produce change or have an effect upon their children. As a former teacher in a Christian school, I was able to observe the defiant behavior of students in the classroom. Going to the principal's office and being sent home only worked for a short period of time. Parents are at their wit's end. They don't know what else to do. Even going to counselors sometimes doesn't help.

Many children end up in a school counselor's office, only to then be sent to a psychiatrist who diagnoses some kind of attention disorder or some other sickness or disorder. After many dollars and hours spent in therapy, as well as many medications prescribed, many parents will say that the situation is not getting any better. I hear parents say, "While he's on medication, I can tolerate him, but once the medication wears off, he becomes a little devil again."

If you are in this situation, let me address these thoughts to you. Make a thorough examination of your heart and thoughts. Are you quick with your tongue? Do you yell and scream when you get angry? Do you fight with your husband in front of the children? Are you always talking negatively? Do you fly off the handle easily? Do you become impatient with the many questions your child asks? Are you a workaholic who cannot make enough time to nurture and spend time with your children? Do you make a habit of going to church on Sundays and taking your child to a Bible class? Do your children watch television unsupervised for many hours at a time? Do you allow violent adult movies in the presence of your children? Is pornography allowed in your home?

There are so many other questions I could ask, but you get the idea I am trying to convey. What you allow in your home and heart is having and will have a tremendous effect upon your family. Children in these situations are experiencing the effects of learned behavioral patterns during childhood. In many instances evil spirits play a big role in the child's behavior.

In order to reverse this pattern, there has to be great change. It begins with you, Mom and Dad. First, there must be repentance from the heart, followed by forsaking the past and allowing God to change and heal you. I greatly recommend that you ask your family members to forgive you of your ignorance and ungodly actions. Forgiveness releases healing and sets captives free.

It will be a process of each day consciously deciding to allow the Holy Spirit to teach you and help you change old habits and patterns of thinking.

I recommend that you begin with the words that you speak. Let them be positive and constructive. When you feel like arguing, stop and willfully decide that you are not going to become upset, but you will have self-control. Make prayer a practice every day. Surrender your life to your heavenly Father, and ask the Holy Spirit to help you in everything you do. Begin the walk to blessings and victories today. Don't put it off for another moment. Your children will see and notice the difference and will imitate you.

As you mature, you will be able to enter into the spiritual warfare this book talks about. Then you will be able to use the keys of binding and loosing, and you will see the strongholds of disobedience and defiance in your children destroyed by God's power. Believe in your heart that as you apply the blood of Jesus, the enemy has to flee from your home. But parents, it first begins with you. Satan does not pay any attention to the commands of someone who is disobedient himself.

"I CAN'T FORGIVE THOSE WHO HURT ME"

It was not my original intention to add this subject to this book. But after completion of my original thoughts, I felt the need to come back and add these thoughts. You will remain a slave to the person or persons for whom you hold a grudge or bitterness unless you willfully forgive them in your heart. Your forgiveness allows the Spirit of God to begin a healing process in you. Many times unforgiveness on the part of parents causes behavior patterns that negatively affect the behavior of the entire family. My own personal freedom began when I first made the decision in my heart to forgive my father. Then I made the spoken declaration. Finally I took action. I went to my father, and I told him that I forgave him. It was not easy, but it turned out to be the most liberating thing that I have ever done. You may not have to face your abuser, but begin in your heart to forgive.

> If you forgive the sins of any, they are forgiven them; if you retain the sins of any, they are *retained*.
> —John 20:23, nkjv, emphasis added

This verse means that if you do not forgive, you *retain* (keep) the person's sin against you in your body and soul. The person whom you will not forgive also remains bound! If you can understand this, you will be set free. *The spirit of unforgiveness cannot be allowed to continue taking root in your life. It will contaminate everything good in your life and family.*

What you are dealing with is a spiritual matter. Evil spirits took control of your abuser and caused him or her to harm and take advantage of you in some way. The Word of God says that our fight is not with humans (flesh and blood), but it is against Satan and his evil forces.

Understand where the attack comes from. Let's look at the following verse:

> For we are not wrestling with flesh and blood [contending only with physical opponents], but against the despotisms, against the powers, against [the master spirits who are] the world rulers of this present darkness, against the spirit forces of wickedness in the heavenly (supernatural) sphere.
>
> —EPHESIANS 6:12, AMP

The attacks come straight out of the kingdom of darkness. The devil rules this kingdom, and he is trying to rule the life of every child of God. Get into action and boldly declare offensive warfare against Satan and his demons. Start offending the enemy with the Word of God. Snatch your children from the destructive grip of Satan. Your power in Christ is greater. Don't be a passive coward any longer. Stop blaming your past and your dysfunctional childhood. Start taking responsibility for your own actions.

Recognize who the real enemy is and resist him. Some of you reading this may not be able to change the attitudes and habits of your children, perhaps because of their ages. Children are not ignorant; they know a change when they see it. They know love and compassion when they see and feel it. Your children will be affected by your love and obedience to God. Add prayers to this warfare, and you will definitely see some life-transforming changes take place. *You cannot allow your position to be weakened by what you see, hear, or know. This is a walk of faith and trust in God.*

You no longer have to live in bondage and bitterness. It is time to release your heavy burden of abuse to God and allow Him to heal you from the inside out. God has made provision for you and equipped you with weapons of warfare. He has given you power over all the power of the enemy. The battle will rage in your mind and manifest in your body and actions. It is about time that you put a stop to these attacks and start living a life of victory and peace in Christ Jesus.

The moment that *you* begin taking a stand against the attacks of the enemy and believe that God will restore you and your family, at that precise moment you will begin to be set free. You will begin to live a new life of victory, peace, and blessing. You will experience the joy of the Lord. It will be a dramatic and life-changing event that will take place. Put your foot down and say, "Enough is enough." When you do that, you will begin a journey toward healing and freedom in Christ.

If your child is a victim of abuse and too young to understand, stand in the gap for that child as you bind the spirits of abuse from tormenting his or her mind and causing fear and disorders. Your prayers are powerful to the pulling down strongholds!

REDEEMED FROM THE CURSE

Because we are redeemed from the curse of the law, we can break the strongholds of generational and inherited curses. Invisible forces are at work that determine a person's destiny. The Bible refers to these forces of good and evil as *blessings* and *curses*. A biblical understanding about this subject will give you the knowledge necessary to set you and your family free from many problems that you have not been able to understand. You will have a new perspective of your own life. I recommend that you seek and apply knowledge and understanding about this subject by reading and studying books by reputable Christian authors. You will be enriched, encouraged, transformed by the Word of God and the insight of godly authors.

Many failures in your life could be the consequence of a family curse passed down through your grandparents and parents from generation to generation. We have been redeemed by the blood of Jesus. All we need to do is take a stand and appropriate our legal rights as children of God. Let the enemy know that you have been set free. He cannot continue putting on you the things from which you have already been set free.

Take a stand, and make your declaration of faith. One example might be the following:

> *By the stripes of Jesus I am healed. No weapon formed against me shall prosper. Satan, you can't have my children. They belong to God, and I claim them for the kingdom of God. I have the mind of Christ, and I bring every thought captive to the obedience of Christ. I will not permit these thoughts to control me in the name of Jesus. I have been set free from lustful and perverted thoughts. I renounce all involvement with the occult,*

whether through my own ignorance or that of my parents. I declare that the curse of divorce will not visit my home or my children and their children. I will continually walk in love.

Satan, I break your strongholds over my family. I give up all my rebellion and all my sin, and I submit myself to the lordship of Jesus Christ. I have been redeemed from every curse!

This sample prayer is only a small example of things that hinder and may be a cause for a curse in your family. Only the power of the Word of God flowing from your lips and heart will set you and your family free. The moment you begin making these declarations, you will put into motion the Word of God on your behalf.

The Word of God says, "They overcame him [Satan] by the blood of the Lamb and by the word of their testimony, and they did not love their lives to the death" (Rev. 12:11, NKJV).

Your declaration of faith together with God's love in action will transform not only you but also those with whom you come into contact. The problem with so many Christians is their ignorance about the kingdom of light. They do not realize they have been created to rule and reign here on this earth as sons and daughters of the King. Instead, the enemy is ruling and reigning in the majority of Christian homes.

The principles, values, and belief system of this world are teaching us to fight for our rights, do what feels good, and make our own decisions. The Word of God gives us a different set of rules and perspective based upon God's love, mercy, and compassion. There's no fight or competition involved in His love. Outside of His love, there are only evil curses. The blessings only belong to those who dare to live and walk in the kingdom of God.

Read and personalize the following scriptures. Break the curse of abuse and other sins in your generation. You are a conqueror! But in order to be a conqueror, you must conquer something. Begin praying right now!

> I call heaven and earth as witnesses today against you, that I have set before you life and death, blessings and cursing; therefore choose life, that both you and your descendants may live.
>
> —Deuteronomy 30:19, nkjv

Here is an example of personalizing this scripture:

> *Father God, You have set life and death, as well as blessings and curses, before us. Today I choose life and blessings. My children and family will serve You. We will live and not die!*

> Christ redeemed us from the curse of the law by becoming a curse for us, for it is written: "Cursed is everyone who is hung on a tree." Christ redeemed us…in order that the blessing given to Abraham might come to the Gentiles through Christ Jesus,

so that by faith we might receive the promise of the Spirit.

—GALATIANS 3:13–14

Thank You, Lord Jesus, for redeeming us from the curse of the law and blessing us as you also blessed Abraham. By faith I receive the promise of the Holy Spirit.

SCRIPTURES RELATED TO DELIVERANCE

I have power over all the power of the enemy.

I have given you authority to trample on snakes and scorpions and to overcome all the power of the enemy; nothing will harm you.

—LUKE 10:19

Submit yourselves, then, to God. Resist the devil, and he will flee from you.

—JAMES 4:7

I [or the name(s) of your child or children] have been delivered from the powers of darkness and the hand of the enemy.

For he has rescued us from the dominion of darkness and brought us into the kingdom of the Son he loves.

—COLOSSIANS 1:13

I will save you from the hands of the wicked and redeem you from the grasp of the cruel.

—Jeremiah 15:21

For God, who said, "Let light shine out of darkness," made his light shine in our hearts to give us the light of the knowledge of the glory of God in the face of Christ.

—2 Corinthians 4:6

I call upon the Lord, and He delivers me!

And everyone who calls on the name of the Lord will be saved; for on Mount Zion and in Jerusalem there will be deliverance, as the Lord has said, among the survivors whom the Lord calls.

—Joel 2:32

The Lord is my hiding place. He will preserve and deliver me.

You are my hiding place; you will protect me from trouble and surround me with songs of deliverance.

—Psalm 32:7

Call upon me in the day of trouble; I will deliver you, and you will honor me.

—Psalm 50:15

I have been redeemed and delivered from the curse of the law. Christ lives in me.

But now, by dying to what once bound us, we have been released from the law so that we serve in the new way of the Spirit, and not in the old way of the written code.

—ROMANS 7:6

The Lord will lead my children out of darkness and into His light!

I will lead the blind by ways they have not known, along unfamiliar paths I will guide them; I will turn the darkness into light before them and make the rough places smooth. These are the things I will do; I will not forsake them.

—ISAIAH 42:16

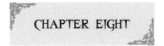

CHAPTER EIGHT

GOD'S PROMISES FOR PARENTS

SCRIPTURE PRAYING FOR CHILDREN
YOUNG AND GROWN

And this is the confidence (the assurance, the privilege of
boldness) which we have in Him: [we are sure] that if we ask any-
thing (make any request) according to His will
(in agreement with His own plan), He listens to and hears us.

—I JOHN 5:14, AMP

PRAYING ACCORDING TO God's Word is one of the most powerful ways you will ever pray. Scripture praying is putting God's Word into action. Open your heart and your mouth, and begin invading the darkness and taking back what rightfully belongs to you! Many of these declarations you will make by faith, believing in those things that are not as though they already are. Personalize these scriptures by adding the person's name.

God is a shield to my children.

Every word of God is flawless; he is a shield to those who take refuge in him.

—PROVERBS 30:5

My children are for signs and wonders.

Here am I, and the children the LORD has given me. We are signs and symbols in Israel from the LORD Almighty, who dwells on Mount Zion.

—ISAIAH 8:18

Children are a reward from God.

Sons are a heritage from the LORD,
    children a reward from him.
Like arrows in the hands of a warrior
    are sons born in one's youth.
Blessed is the man
    whose quiver is full of them.
They will not be put to shame
    when they contend with their enemies in the gate.

—PSALM 127:3–5

God's covenant to me and to my children is everlasting.

I will establish my covenant as an everlasting covenant between me and you and your descendants after you for the generations to come, to be your God and the God of your descendants after you.

—Genesis 17:7

God's mercy is everlasting.

But from everlasting to everlasting the Lord's love is with those who fear him, and his righteousness with their children's children.

—Psalm 103:17

God's angels are always near my children.

Praise the Lord, you his angels, you mighty ones who do his bidding, who obey his word.

—Psalm 103:20

My children shall praise Him.

From the lips of children and infants you have ordained praise because of your enemies, to silence the foe and the avenger.

—Psalm 8:2

Lord, protect my children from temptation.

For we do not have a high priest who is unable to sympathize with our weaknesses, but we have one who has been tempted in every way, just as we are—yet was without sin.

—Hebrews 4:15

Lord, perform Your Word in their lives.

The Lord said to me, "You have seen correctly, for I am watching to see that my word is fulfilled."

—Jeremiah 1:12

God's Word shall not return void.

So is my word that goes out from my mouth: It will not return to me empty, but will accomplish what I desire and achieve the purpose for which I sent it.

—Isaiah 55:11

My children will be restored.

I will repay you for the years the locusts have eaten—the great locust and the young locust, the other locusts and the locust swarm—my great army that I sent among you.

—Joel 2:25

As I declare it, God will establish it.

What you decide on will be done, and light will shine on your ways.

—Job 22:28

Nothing shall harm my family or me.

He replied, "I saw Satan fall like lightning from heaven. I have given you authority to trample on snakes and scorpions and to overcome all the power of the enemy; nothing will harm you."

—Luke 10:18–19

God gives me strength and power.

You are awesome, O God, in your sanctuary; the God of Israel gives power and strength to his people. Praise be to God!

—Psalm 68:35

God Almighty will save my children.

But this is what the Lord says: "Yes, captives will be taken from warriors, and plunder retrieved from the fierce; I will contend with those who contend with you, and your children I will save."

—Isaiah 49:25

My children will come back to God and their family.

Lift up your eyes and look about you: All assemble and come to you; your sons come from afar, and your daughters are carried on the arm.

—Isaiah 60:4

My children belong to the kingdom of God.

They replied, "Believe in the Lord Jesus, and you will be saved—you and your household."

—Acts 16:31

Great is the peace of my children.

All your sons will be taught by the Lord, and great will be your children's peace.

—Isaiah 54:13

My children will prophesy and see visions from God.

And afterward, I will pour out my Spirit on all people. Your sons and daughters will prophesy, your old men will dream dreams, your young men will see visions.

—Joel 2:28

My children will delight in the Lord.

Delight yourself in the LORD and he will give you the desires of your heart.

—PSALM 37:4

Help me, Lord, to train my children; my children shall not depart from God.

Train up a child in the way he should go, and when he is old he will not depart from it.

—PROVERBS 22:6, NKJV

Lord, keep my children strong in faith.

Yet he did not waver through unbelief regarding the promise of God, but was strengthened in his faith and gave glory to God.

—ROMANS 4:20

My children shall not perish.

In the same way your Father in heaven is not willing that any of these little ones should be lost.

—MATTHEW 18:14

God sees my tears and hears my cries.

Those who sow with tears
    will reap with songs of joy.
He who goes out weeping,
    carrying seed to sow,
will return with songs of joy,
    carrying sheaves with him.

—Psalm 126:5–6

The Lord shall increase in my children.

May the Lord make you increase, both you and your children.

—Psalm 115:14

My children are called and chosen by God.

Listen to me, you islands; hear this, you distant nations: Before I was born the Lord called me; from my birth he has made mention of my name.

—Isaiah 49:1

The Lord will bless and multiply my family.

He will love you and bless you and increase your numbers. He will bless the fruit of your womb, the crops of your land—your grain, new wine and olive oil—the calves of your herds and the lambs of your flocks in the land that he swore to your forefathers to give you.

—Deuteronomy 7:13

The Lord will perfect that which concerns my family.

The Lord will perfect that which concerns me; Your mercy, O Lord, endures forever; do not forsake the works of Your hands.

—Psalm 138:8, nkjv

God fulfills all things for me according to His Word.

I will cry out to God Most High, to God who performs all things for me.

—Psalm 57:2, nkjv

My children are blessed.

He strengthens the bars of your gates and blesses your people within you.

—Psalm 147:13

*My children shall come back from the land of the
enemy! I have great hope!*

This is what the LORD says:

"Restrain your voice from weeping
    and your eyes from tears,
for your work will be rewarded,"
    declares the Lord.
   "They will return from the land of the enemy.
So there is hope for your future,"
    declares the LORD.
   "Your children will return to their own land."
                —JEREMIAH 31:16–17

*Father, I covenant that the Word of God will not
depart from my mouth or the mouths of my children.*

"As for me, this is my covenant with them," says the
LORD. "My Spirit, who is on you, and my words that
I have put in your mouth will not depart from your
mouth, or from the mouths of your children, or from
the mouths of their descendants from this time on
and forever," says the LORD.

                —ISAIAH 59:21

PRAYER OF FAITH

Dear God, please help my children navigate through all the hard places in life—through the pitfalls, the holes, the stumbling blocks, the peer pressures, the pleasures and temptations, the fearful places, and the areas of decision.

Keep their heart toward You, Lord, I pray. Please remove the bands from their eyes and the veils from their hearts. Cause them to seek You with all their heart.

I bind the unclean spirits and the spirits of fear and rejection from attaching themselves to them. I loose the love and peace of God into their hearts.

Thank You, Father, for placing a hedge of protection around them. Thank You for sending Your angels to protect and deliver them from all evil.

In Jesus's name, amen.

Remember, the miracle is in your mouth!

MY IDENTITY AND POSITION IN CHRIST

+ I am a child of God and one with Christ (John 1:12).

+ I am an overcomer in this world (1 John 4:4).

+ The Word is medicine and health to all my body (Prov. 4:20–22).

- I am born of God, and the evil one cannot touch me (1 John 5:18).

- I am the salt of the earth (Matt. 5:13).

- I am the light of the world (Matt. 5:14).

- I am a new creation (2 Cor. 5:17).

- I am united in Christ, and I am one spirit with Him (1 Cor. 6:17).

- I am a partaker of the heavenly calling (Heb. 3:1).

- I can do all things through Christ who gives me the strength (Phil. 4:13).

- I am chosen by God to produce fruit (John 15:16).

- I am an heir and joint-heir with Christ Jesus (Rom. 8:17).

- I am an enemy of the devil (1 Pet. 5:8).

- I am crucified with Christ, and sin has no dominion over me (Rom. 6:1–6).

- I have the mind of Christ (1 Cor. 2:16).

+ I am healed by the stripes of Jesus (1 Pet. 2:24).

+ I am prosperous as my soul prospers, and I walk in health (3 John 2).

+ No weapon formed against me shall prosper (Isa. 54:17).

+ I am a citizen of heaven (Eph. 2:6).

+ I am a member of the body of Christ (1 Cor. 12:27).

+ I am God's temple, and the Holy Spirit dwells in me (1 Cor. 3:16; 6:19).

+ My life is hidden in Christ (Col. 3:3).

+ I am justified by faith, and I have peace with God (Rom. 5:1).

+ The law of the Spirit of life in Christ has set me free from the law of sin and death (Rom. 8:2).

+ I am redeemed and forgiven through the blood of Jesus (Eph. 1:6–8).

- I do not have a spirit of fear but of God's power (the Holy Spirit) and His love. I have a sound mind (2 Tim. 1:7).

- I am complete in Christ (Col. 2:10).

- I am blessed with every spiritual blessing (Eph. 1:3).

- I am free forever from condemnation (Rom. 8:1).

- I am established, anointed, and sealed in Christ (2 Cor. 1:21–22).

- I have access to my heavenly Father through Christ Jesus (Eph. 2:18).

- I have access to the Father through faith in Him (Eph. 3:12).

- I have forgiveness of sins through the blood of Christ (Col. 1:14).

- All my needs are met according to His riches in glory (Phil. 4:19).

PRAYER FOR DESPONDENT AND REBELLIOUS CHILDREN

Dear Father God,

My children are lost and without Your protection and guidance. Your Word declares, "Believe in the Lord Jesus, and you will be saved—you and your household" (Acts 16:31).

Lord, Your promises never change. I rebuke the works of the enemy in my children's lives, and in the name of Jesus I come against all the strongholds of the enemy against my family. I come against all evil spirits that keep my children bound, confused, full of unbelief, and unwilling to give their lives to the will of God.

I bind their will to the will of God and to the truth in God's Word. Thank You, Lord, for Your promise in Matthew 16:19 that everything we bind on earth will be bound in heaven, and everything we loose on earth will be loosed in heaven.

I declare that my children and my family will serve You. Father, I declare that I will stand fast in Your liberty and not be entangled again with the yoke of bondage, as Galatians 5:1 states. I thank You for setting us free and redeeming us with the blood of Jesus.

In the name of Jesus, amen.

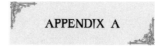

DECLARATION OF FAITH

I N THE NAME of Jesus, I resist the enemy, and he must flee from me. I yield myself to the power of Jesus Christ as my Lord and Savior.

I claim my union with Christ through His death and resurrection.

I bind the works of the enemy from interfering in my life and family.

I plead the blood of Jesus over my family and declare that God has given me power and authority over all the power of the enemy. Nothing shall harm us (Luke 10:19).

I bring every thought and imagination in my mind captive to the obedience of Christ. I will think on those things that are pure and of a good report (Phil. 4:8).

Your Word declares that You will never leave us or forsake us. I will not fear or be dismayed, for You are my help and my fortress. You will strengthen and harden me to difficulties. You will hold me up and retain me with Your right hand of rightness and justice (Isa. 41:10).

I thank You, my Father, for loving me and caring about my family. I rejoice in Your faithfulness and unconditional love for us.

In Jesus's name, amen.

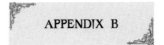

PRAYER TO RECEIVE JESUS CHRIST AS LORD AND SAVIOR

THE BIBLE SAYS:

That is you confess with your mouth, "Jesus is Lord," and believe in your heart that God raised him from the dead, you will be saved. For it is with your heart that you believe and are justified, and it is with your mouth that you confess and are saved.

—ROMANS 10:9–10

To receive Jesus Christ as the Lord and Savior of your life, pray this prayer with all your heart:

Lord Jesus,

I desire to know You personally. Thank You for dying for me on the cross to redeem my sins. I open the door of my life and heart and receive You as my Lord and Savior. Thank You for forgiving all of my sins and giving me eternal life. Please take control of my life and help me to overcome.

In Jesus's name, amen.

Once you have prayed this prayer, sign below and date your signature.

SIGNATURE _____

DATE _____

CONTACT INFORMATION

I RIS DELGADO AND her husband, John Delgado, are confer-
ence speakers and teachers, specializing in family, marriage,
parenting, and leadership conferences and seminars. E-mail
them or visit their websites for more information.

E-mail

info@crownedwithpurpose.com

johndelgado@gmail.com

Websites

www.crownedwithpurpose.com

www.viu.cc